	DATE DUE		

D0845628

Using and Understanding Maps

Population of the World

Consulting Editor
Scott E. Morris
College of Mines and Earth Resources
University of Idaho

Chelsea House Publishers
New York   Philadelphia

This Publication was designed, edited and computer generated by Lovell Johns Limited
10 Hanborough Business Park
Long Hanborough
Witney
Oxon, England OX8 8LH

The contents of this volume are based on the latest data available at the _time of publication.

Map credit: *Antarctica source map prepared at 1:20,000 by the British Antarctic Survey Mapping and Geographic Information Centre, 1990.*

Cover credit: *Harold and Erica Van Pelt, Photographers, Los Angeles.*

Printed in Mexico

3 5 7 9 8 6 4 2

Library of Congress Cataloging in Publication Data

Populations of the world/editorial consultant, Scott Morris:
    p. cm.—(Using and understanding maps)
    Includes glossary and index/gazetteer.
    Includes bibliographical references.
    Summary: Eighteen map spreads present information about
    where the various peoples of the world live.
    ISBN 0-7910-1805-9. — ISBN 0-7910-1818-0 (pbk.)
    1. Population— Maps. [1. Population—Maps. 2. Atlases]
    I. Morris, Scott Edward. II. Chelsea House Publishers. III. Series.
    G1046.E2P6 1993 <G&M>
    304.6' .022' 3 — dc20   92-22283
                                          CIP
                                          MAP AC

Introduction

We inhabit a fascinating and mysterious planet where the earth's physical features, life-forms, and the diversity of human culture conspire to produce a breathtaking environment. We don't have to travel very far to see and experience the wealth of this diverse planet; in fact, we don't have to travel at all. Everywhere images of the world are abundantly available in books, newspapers, magazines, movies, television, and the arts. We could say that *everywhere* one looks, our world is a brilliant moving tapestry of shapes, colors, and textures, and our experience of its many messages — whether in our travels or simply by gazing out into our own backyards — is what we call reality.

Geography is the study of a portion of that reality. More so, it is the study of how the physical and biological components (rocks, animals, plants, and people) of our planet are distributed and how they are interconnected. Geographers seek to describe and to explain the physical patterns that have evolved on the earth and also to discover the significance in the ways they have evolved. To do this, geographers rely on maps.

Maps can be powerful images. They convey selective information about vast areas of an overwhelmingly cluttered world. The cartographer, or mapmaker, must carefully choose the theme of a map, that is, what it will show, knowing that a good map will convey the essence of information while at the same time making the information easy to comprehend.

This volume and its companions in UNDERSTANDING AND USING MAPS are about the planet we call earth and the maps we use to find our way along its peaks and valleys. Each volume displays map images that reveal how the world is arranged according to a specific theme such as population, industries or the endangered world. The maps in each volume are accompanied by an interesting collection of facts — some are rather obvious, others are oddities. Yet all are meant to be informative.

Along with a wealth of facts, there are explanations of the various attributes and phenomena depicted by the maps. This information is provided to better understand the significance of the maps as well as to demonstrate how the many themes relate.

Names for places are essential to geographers. To study the world without devising names for places would be extremely difficult. But geographers also know that names are in no way permanent; place names change as people change. The recent reunification of Germany and the breakup of what was the Soviet Union — events that seem colossal from the perspective of socioeconomics — to geographers are simply events that require the drawing or erasing of one or a few boundaries and the renaming of one or several land masses. The geographer is constantly reminded that the world is in flux; a map is always in danger of being rendered obsolete by a turn in current events.

Because the world is dynamic, it continues to captivate the mind and stimulate the imagination. USING AND UNDERSTANDING MAPS presents the world as it is today, with the reservation that any dramatic rearrangement of land and people is likely, indeed inevitable, thus requiring the making of a new map. In this way maps are themselves a part of the evolutionary process.

Scott E. Morris

Population of the World

Today, there are 3 people born every second, and at that rate, there will be 1 billion new residents of the earth in the next 10 years. By the year 2025, global population is projected to be 8.5 billion. These people will need food, shelter, and clothing: essentials that must be provided by our small planet. Many experts believe that the single most important task facing the world today is reining in population growth.

Why is the earth's population growing so fast? Population grows when the number of births in a given year exceeds the number of deaths. Population decreases when the birth rate is less than the death rate. Because different countries have different birth and death rates, population growth varies widely between countries. Demographers, people who study population trends, indicate that present-day growth rates are highest in LDCs (less developed countries). The LDCs include many of the nations of Africa, Asia, and Latin America.

In the LDCs, the death rate has, traditionally, been quite high; life posed many hazards. The high death rate "allowed" a high birth rate without causing population growth. During the past 50 years however, unprecedented progress has been made in sanitation, medicine, and education, and these improvements have caused a dramatic decline in the death rate. At the same time, the birth rates in most of these countries have remained high. Each year more and more men and women reach reproductive age. The large number of young people having many children produces a rapidly growing population.

This growth is especially troublesome because it is occurring in the very countries that are struggling to provide for their existing population. The situation is often made worse by population movement. In 1900, only 14 percent of the world's population lived in cities. Today, nearly one-half do. In the LDCs more than 20 million people move to the cities each year. Most often, the cities cannot provide services for these people. They end up illegally "squatting" on private land, living in makeshift shantytowns with no running water or sanitation facilities.

Even in the MDCs (more developed countries) (such as the United States, Japan, and most of the European nations), the same population shift to the cities has had negative effects. Air and water pollution, waste disposal crises, crime, unemployment, and racial and ethnic tensions all plague our cities. Things that have traditionally been taken for granted — abundant drinking water, safe roads and bridges, adequate power supplies — are threatened by the crush of people.

The solution to these problems begins with education. In countries with high birth rates, governments need to educate their people and provide economic rewards for responsible family planning. Such family programs are, themselves, important efforts, as are programs to increase the educational and employment opportunities for women throughout the world. In the MDCs, the population must be educated to use less of the world's resources and decrease damage to the environment. Developed countries account for only 25 percent of the world's population, yet they use 80 percent of the world's resources. We all have an obligation to our fellow citizens. These maps, and the text and statistics that accompany them, are a beginning in the educational process.

Scott E. Morris

gend lists and explains the symbols and colors
d on the map. It is called a legend because it
s the story of a map. It is important to read the
legend to find out exactly what the symbols
n because some symbols do not look like
t they represent. For example, a dot stands
a town.
ry map in this atlas has a legend on it.

This legend lists and explains the colors and
symbols used on the map on that page only.
The legend on the left, below, shows examples of the
colors used on the maps in all the atlases in this
series. Below this is a list of all symbols used on the
maps in all the atlases in this series.
The legend on the right, below, is an example of a
legend used in the physical atlas.

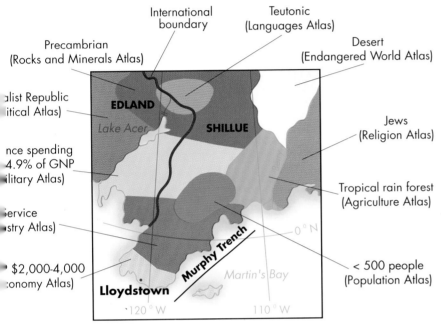

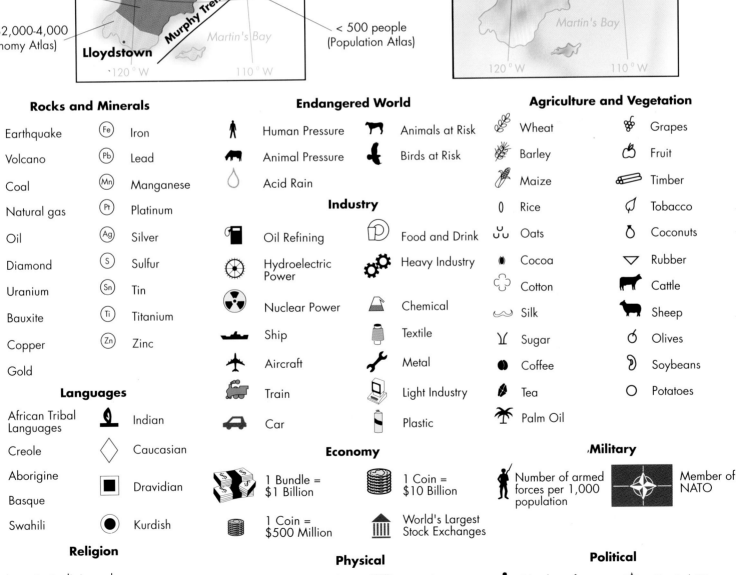

Rocks and Minerals

Earthquake	(Fe)	Iron
Volcano	(Pb)	Lead
Coal	(Mn)	Manganese
Natural gas	(Pt)	Platinum
Oil	(Ag)	Silver
Diamond	(S)	Sulfur
Uranium	(Sn)	Tin
Bauxite	(Ti)	Titanium
Copper	(Zn)	Zinc
Gold		

Languages

African Tribal Languages		Indian
Creole		Caucasian
Aborigine		Dravidian
Basque		
Swahili		Kurdish

Religion

Important religious place

Endangered World

Human Pressure		Animals at Risk
Animal Pressure		Birds at Risk
Acid Rain		

Industry

Oil Refining		Food and Drink
Hydroelectric Power		Heavy Industry
Nuclear Power		Chemical
Ship		Textile
Aircraft		Metal
Train		Light Industry
Car		Plastic

Economy

1 Bundle = $1 Billion	1 Coin = $10 Billion
1 Coin = $500 Million	World's Largest Stock Exchanges

Physical

Mountain Peak	Canal

Agriculture and Vegetation

Wheat		Grapes
Barley		Fruit
Maize		Timber
Rice		Tobacco
Oats		Coconuts
Cocoa		Rubber
Cotton		Cattle
Silk		Sheep
Sugar		Olives
Coffee		Soybeans
Tea		Potatoes
Palm Oil		

Military

Number of armed forces per 1,000 population	Member of NATO

Political

Number of Political Parties	Capital City

World Physical

This page is a physical map of the world. It indicates where the major physical features — such as mountain ranges, plains, deserts, lakes, and rivers — are in the world. As the world is very large, the map has to be drawn at a very small scale in order to fit onto a page. This map is drawn at a scale so that 1 inch on the map, at the equator, equals 1,840 miles on the ground.

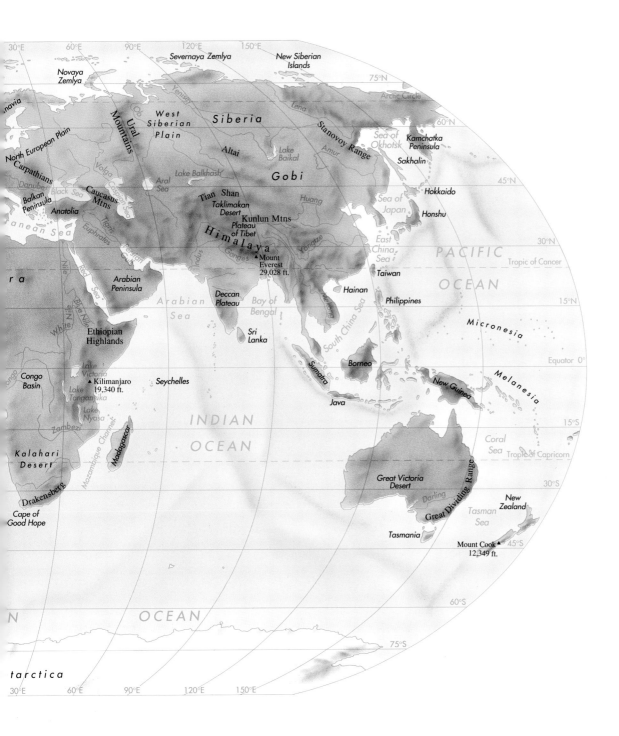

30°E 60°E 90°E 120°E 150°E

Severnaya Zemlya

New Siberian Islands

Novaya Zemlya

75°N

Arctic Circle

-navia

West Siberian Plain

Siberia

60°N

Ural Mountains

Ob

Yenisey

Lena

Stanovoy Range

Sea of Okhotsk

Kamchatka Peninsula

North European Plain

Altai

Lake Baikal

Gobi

Amur

Sakhalin

45°N

Carpathians

Volga

Lake Balkhash

Huang

Sea of Japan

Hokkaido

Danube

Aral Sea

Caspian Sea

Tian Shan

Honshu

Balkan Peninsula

Black Sea

Caucasus Mtns

Taklimakan Desert

Kunlun Mtns

-anean Sea

Anatolia

Tigris

Euphrates

Plateau of Tibet

Himalaya

Yangtze

East China Sea

30°N

PACIFIC

Nile

Red Sea

Indus

Ganges

▲Mount Everest 29,028 ft.

Taiwan

Tropic of Cancer

-r a

Arabian Peninsula

Deccan Plateau

Bay of Bengal

Hainan

Philippines

OCEAN

15°N

Blue Nile

Arabian Sea

South China Sea

Micronesia

Ethiopian Highlands

White Nile

Sri Lanka

Equator 0°

Congo Basin

Lake Victoria

▲Kilimanjaro 19,340 ft.

Seychelles

Sumatra

Borneo

New Guinea

Melanesia

Lake Tanganyika

Lake Nyasa

Java

Zambezi

INDIAN

15°S

Mozambique Channel

Madagascar

OCEAN

Coral Sea

Tropic of Capricorn

Kalahari Desert

Great Victoria Desert

Great Dividing Range

30°S

Drakensberg

Darling

New Zealand

Cape of Good Hope

Tasman Sea

Tasmania

Mount Cook ▲ 12,349 ft.

45°S

60°S

N

OCEAN

75°S

-tarctica

30°E 60°E 90°E 120°E 150°E

World Key Map

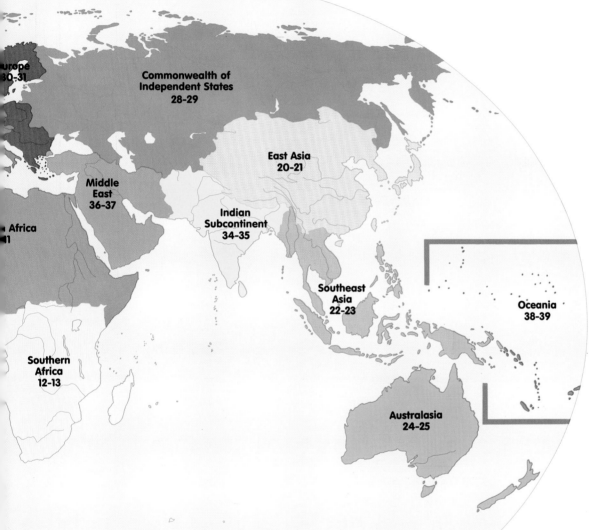

The population of the world is growing rapidly. We share the Earth and its resources with about 250,000 more people every day. The highest growth rates are in the developing countries, especially Africa.

Population Growth Rates

Population growth rates — the percentage of change over time — have peaked everywhere except in Africa.

While the world's population is still growing (nearly 95 million people are added each year), the annual growth rate has slowed from 2.06 per cent in 1965–70 to 1.73 per cent in 1985–90.

But in absolute terms, the world's population is increasing rapidly and will continue to do so well into the 21st century.

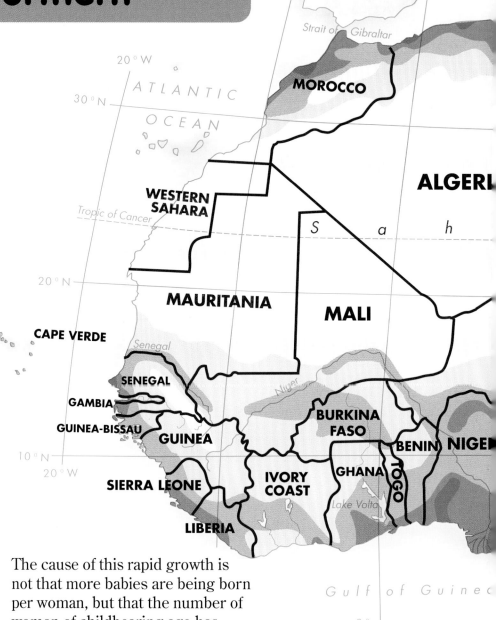

The cause of this rapid growth is not that more babies are being born per woman, but that the number of women of childbearing age has increased rapidly. This bulge in the number of younger people in the age structure of populations is most pronounced in developing countries, and is the result of previous rapid growth rates.

Historically, population growth rates were low because most societies had both high birth rates and high death rates. When there was only a small difference in number between those being born and those dying, populations grew slowly. After World War II many ideas and technologies were introduced into developing countries, affecting health, sanitation, medicine, and education. Death rates fell rapidly, but the traditionally high birth rates continued unchanged.

What the colors and symbols mean

Number of people per square mile

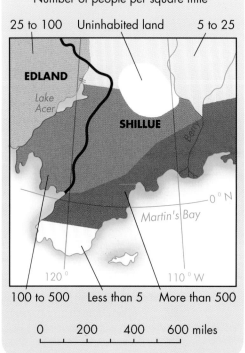

25 to 100	Uninhabited land	5 to 25
100 to 500	Less than 5	More than 500

0   200   400   600 miles

Fewest hospital beds per person

Bangladesh

Afghanistan

Ethiopia

Mali

Nigeria

= 500 people per bed

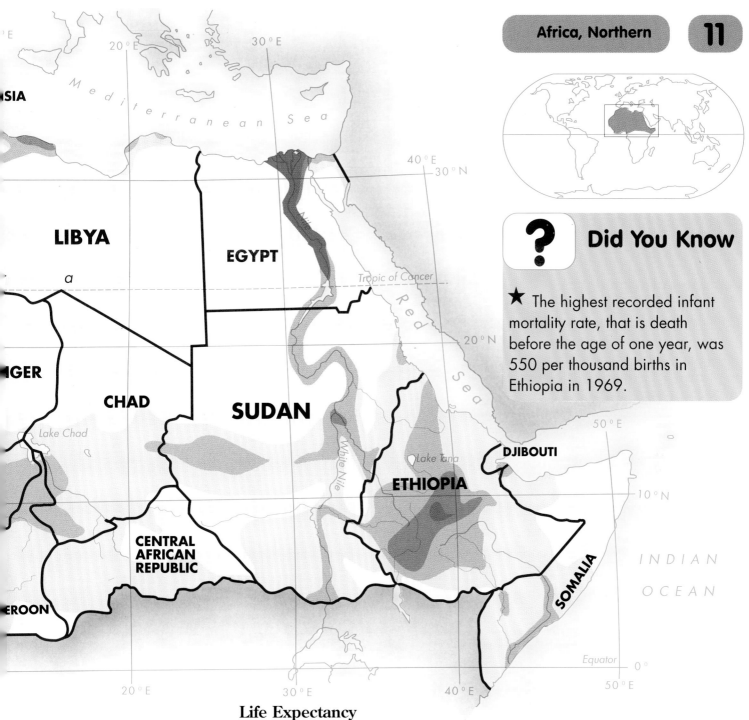

Did You Know

★ The highest recorded infant mortality rate, that is death before the age of one year, was 550 per thousand births in Ethiopia in 1969.

LIBYA

EGYPT

GER

CHAD

SUDAN

Lake Chad

CENTRAL
AFRICAN
REPUBLIC

EROON

DJIBOUTI

ETHIOPIA

Lake Tana

SOMALIA

INDIAN

OCEAN

Tropic of Cancer

Red Sea

White Nile

Equator

Life Expectancy

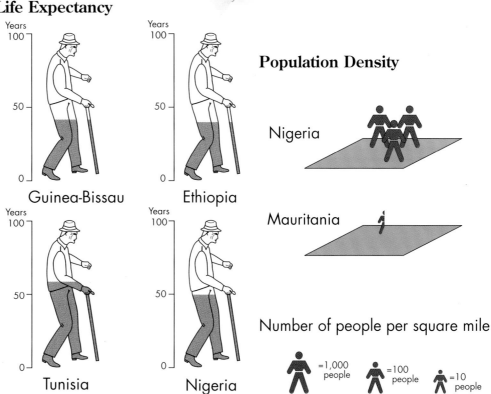

Guinea-Bissau

Ethiopia

Tunisia

Nigeria

Population Density

Nigeria

Mauritania

Number of people per square mile

= 1,000 people   = 100 people   = 10 people

y death rates are near their
ipated minimum, and birth
have started to decline in
countries. If these trends
nue, population growth will
tually return to its traditional
ate, and in the 21st century
and death rates will be
lized at new low levels.

ever, this is not all of the story.
y youthful population such as
nd in developing countries, or
ging population such as is
d in most industrialized
tries, has special implications
ture population growth and for
ocial needs of the country.

The age structure of the population is the pattern created when people are grouped chronologically. The chart for Africa is dominated by the younger age groups. This youthful tilt gets more pronounced in each succeeding time period as more women reach childbearing age.

Population Pyramids

The age structure of a population can be found when the number of people in each age range, such as 0–5, 5–10, 10–15, is calculated. The pattern that emerges is a picture of the distribution of the population at each given age.

In a western industrialized country, for example, the pattern for 1985 would reveal a fairly flat picture, indicating about equal numbers of people in each age range, except for the very old and for the 30–35 and 35–40 age ranges, where there is a distinct bulge known as the postwar baby boom.

However, the 1985 age structure for a developing country, such as one in Central America, would show a pattern that has more people of the younger ages.

While every country has its own pattern, two patterns are common around the world, one for developing countries and one for industrialized countries.

Amazing – But True

★ Kenya's birth rate is twice as high as the worldwide average.

Population Pyramids

Developing

Males   Females

80+
70-80
60-70
50-60
40-50
30-40
20-30
10-20
0-10

16 12 8 4 0 % 0 4 8 12 16

Developed

Males   Females

80+
70-80
60-70
50-60
40-50
30-40
20-30
10-20
0-10

8 4 0 % 0 4 8

What the colors and symbols mean

Number of people per square mile

25 to 100   Uninhabited land   5 to 25

EDLAND

Lake Acer

SHILLUE

Martin's Bay

120°   110° W

100 to 500   Less than 5   More than 500

0   200   400   600 miles

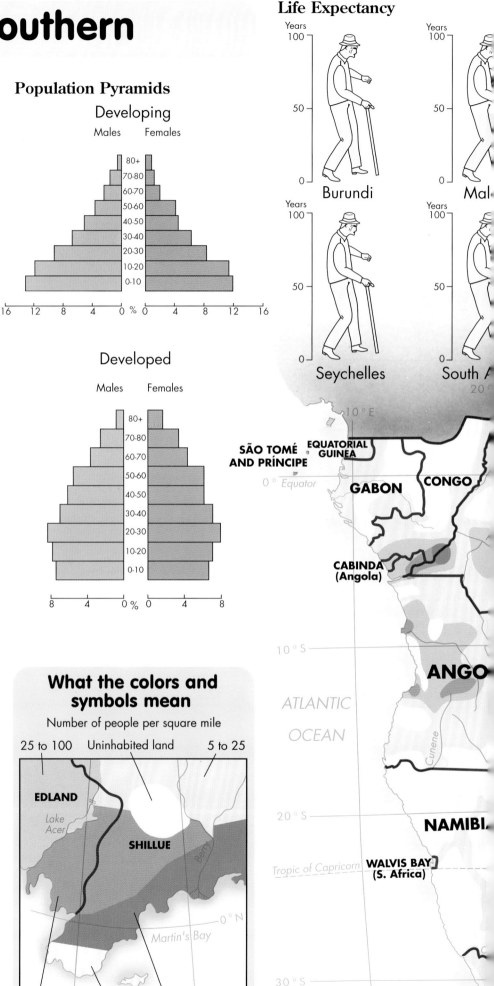

Life Expectancy

Years 100

50

0

Burundi

Years 100

50

0

Mal

Years 100

50

0

Seychelles

Years 100

50

0

South A

10° E

SÃO TOMÉ AND PRÍNCIPE

EQUATORIAL GUINEA

0° Equator

GABON

CONGO

CABINDA (Angola)

10° S

ANGO

ATLANTIC OCEAN

20° S

NAMIBI

Tropic of Capricorn

WALVIS BAY (S. Africa)

Cunene

30° S

10° E

...ulation Density

...auritius

...amibia

...ber of people per square mile

- = 1,000 people
- = 100 people
- = 10 people

Safe Drinking Water

Angola — 100% / 50% / 0%

Botswana — 100% / 50% / 0%

Kenya — 100% / 50% / 0%

Zambia — 100% / 50% / 0%

Zimbabwe — 100% / 50% / 0%

Highest fertility rates

Rwanda

Kenya

Ivory Coast

Zambia

Oman

= 1% of women pregnant

The population of Africa is dominated by a high proportion of the young. This results from a high birth rate that continued despite the fall in the death rate. The gap is projected to continue to widen until at least the year 2000 because the death rate is falling faster than the birth rate. The African population increased at an average annual rate of 2.2% in 1950–55, rising to 2.7% 1970–75 and 3% in 1985–90. It is projected to fall only slightly in the next five year period.

Some 34 million births annually are projected for Africa by the year 2000, compared with 18 million in 1975 and 11 million in 1950.

By 2020, Africa is projected to have reached its anticipated minimum death rate (7 per thousand) and additional drops in the birth rate should then cut deeply into population growth. However, Africa's population will continue to increase rapidly because of the massive increase in the numbers of women of childbearing age.

UGANDA · KENYA · Lake Turkana · Lake Victoria · ...AIRE · RWANDA · BURUNDI · TANZANIA · Lake Tanganyika · ZAMBIA · MALAWI · Lake Nyasa · Ruvuma · MOZAMBIQUE · Zambezi · Lake Kariba · ZIMBABWE · ...WANA · Limpopo · Vaal · SWAZILAND · LESOTHO · ...UTH ...ICA · SEYCHELLES · INDIAN OCEAN · COMOROS · Mozambique Channel · MADAGASCAR · MAURITIUS · Tropic of Capricorn · Equator · 30°E · 40°E · 50°E · 0° · 10°S · 20°S

The rapid movement toward urbanization is most apparent in this area as it has the largest percentage of urban dwellers in the world. Much of the region's future population growth will take place in cities.

Urbanization

An almost universal trend in world population is the growing proportion of town dwellers. It is generally caused by immigrants from the countryside looking for jobs and better living standards in cities. Migration results in a higher birth rate, higher chances of survival, and a declining death rate — though the awful shantytowns of South America and elsewhere are proof that urban life has its own serious problems.

The drift from the country to the town was going on in Europe many centuries ago. The industrialization of the 19th century turned a gentle drift of people into a massive torrent. This trend has now slowed, but it still continues.

? Did You Know

★ One fifth of all Mexicans live in their biggest city, Mexico City.

★ The world's fastest - growing city is Mexico City.

★ A third of the world's people live in towns.

★ The daily increase in the world's population is 223,285, or 155 babies per minute.

Population Density

Barbados

Belize

Number of people per square m

= 1,000 people

= 100 people

= 10 peo

World's Largest Cities

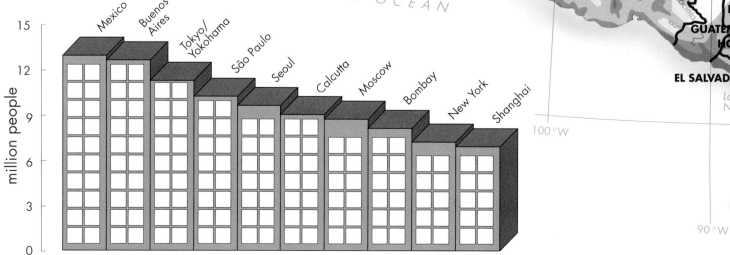

Safe Drinking Water

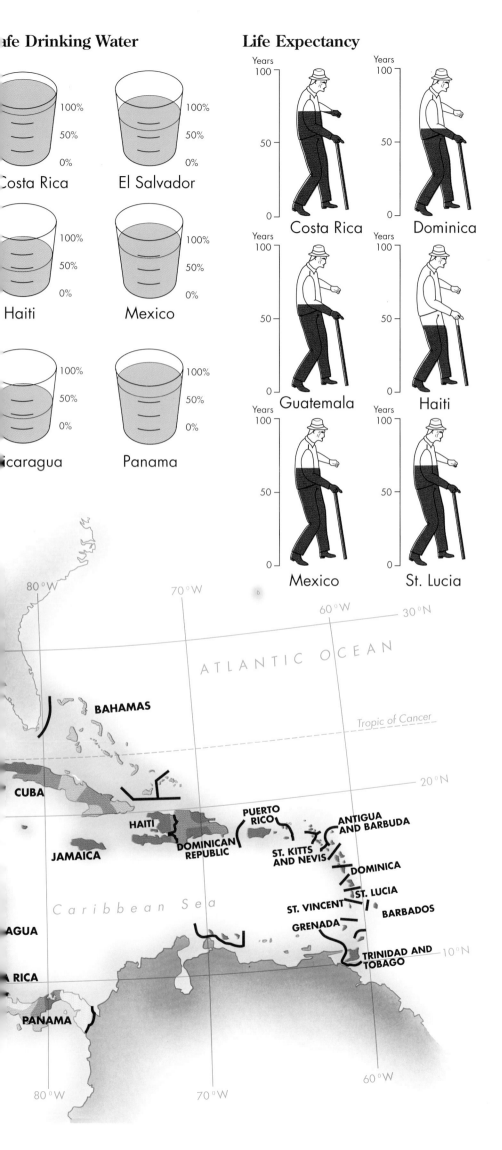

100%
50%
0%
Costa Rica

100%
50%
0%
El Salvador

100%
50%
0%
Haiti

100%
50%
0%
Mexico

100%
50%
0%
Nicaragua

100%
50%
0%
Panama

Life Expectancy

Years
100

50

0
Costa Rica

Years
100

50

0
Dominica

Years
100

50

0
Guatemala

Years
100

50

0
Haiti

Years
100

50

0
Mexico

Years
100

50

0
St. Lucia

Central America

The pattern of age distribution in Central America is similar to that in Africa, though less extreme. The population under the age of 15 years is a substantial percentage of the total (41% in 1950 and 1975).

Since the early 1980s the fertility rate has declined more rapidly than had been predicted, but because of the large number of young women entering their childbearing years the population increases tend to be significant.

Central America had the world's highest growth rate in the period from 1950 to 1975. The population increased by 2.8% per year at its peak. There are marked variations in this area, however. Argentina's population increased very moderately, while Mexico's population increased at a staggering rate of 3.3%.

ATLANTIC OCEAN

30°N

BAHAMAS

Tropic of Cancer

20°N

CUBA

PUERTO RICO

ANTIGUA AND BARBUDA

HAITI

DOMINICAN REPUBLIC

ST. KITTS AND NEVIS

DOMINICA

JAMAICA

ST. LUCIA

ST. VINCENT

BARBADOS

Caribbean Sea

GRENADA

AGUA

TRINIDAD AND TOBAGO

10°N

RICA

PANAMA

80°W

70°W

60°W

70°W

80°W

What the colors and symbols mean

Number of people per square mile

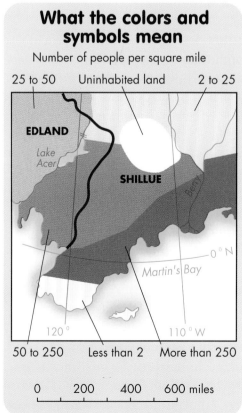

25 to 50	Uninhabited land	2 to 25

EDLAND

Lake Acer

SHILLUE

Berg

0°N

Martin's Bay

120°

110°W

50 to 250	Less than 2	More than 250

0   200   400   600 miles

Megacities are growing rapidly in number and size. One of the biggest is São Paulo, Brazil. Desperately overcrowded slums and squatter settlements are straining health, communications, and sanitation systems to their limit.

Implications of Population Growth

The consequences of population growth can no longer just be seen as problems of food shortages and shortages of land for agriculture. Most of the growth is predicted to occur in cities, which means the continuing growth of megacities and all the problems that go with urban overcrowding. The maturing of the young population will lead to a huge increase in the number of jobs needed, again mainly in urban areas.

Countries heavily dependent on earning money from natural resources will need a rapid exploitation of these, perhaps leading to lasting damage to forests, soils, and mineral resources.

In 1950 less than 30% of the world's population was urban. It is estimated that more than 60% will be urban by 2025. City services will be hard pressed to provide shelter and basic requirements, such as sanitation and water.

The developed world had an urban population of 53% in 1950. This had increased to 73% in 1990 and is predicted to increase only slightly, to 79%, by the year 2025. Central America was 72% urbanized in 1990, but urbanization is predicted to rise to 85% in 2025. Mexico, Colombia, and Brazil tended to have the largest increases in urbanization. Several huge cities have emerged.

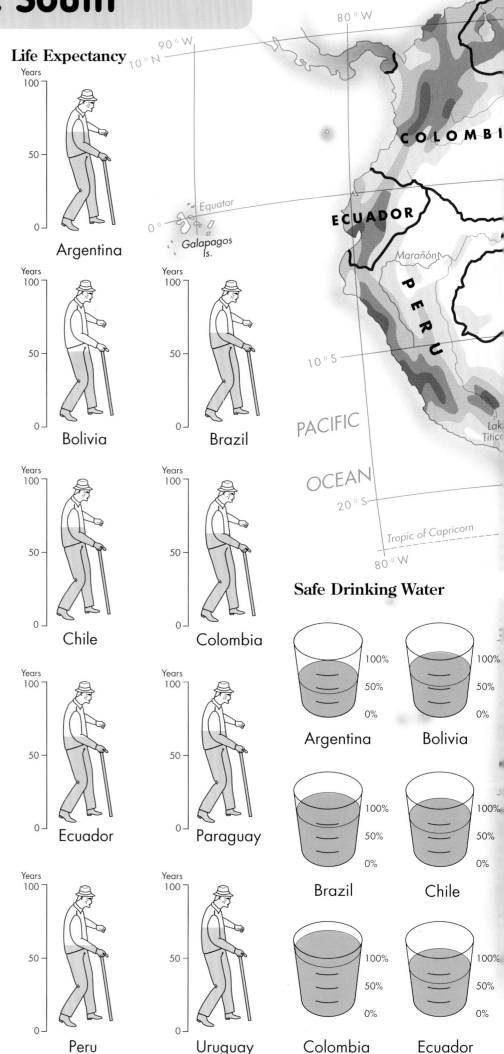

Life Expectancy

Argentina

Bolivia

Brazil

Chile

Colombia

Ecuador

Paraguay

Peru

Uruguay

Safe Drinking Water

Argentina

Bolivia

Brazil

Chile

Colombia

Ecuador

NEZUELA

GUYANA

SURINAME FRENCH GUIANA

Amazon

B R A Z I L

Equator 0°

Tocantins

10°S

OLIVIA

20°S

Paraná

PARAGUAY

São Paulo
Tropic of Capricorn

Paraná

30°S

40°W

URUGUAY
Buenos Aires

ATLANTIC OCEAN

40°S

Population Density

Ecuador

Suriname

50°S

Scotia Sea

Number of people per square mile

= 1,000 people   = 100 people   = 10 people

The Informal Sector

The huge growth in Third World cities creates extraordinary demands for housing, services, and jobs — demands exceeding the capability of most cities to fulfill. The urban poor tend to build settlements on vacant land and to subsist through a wide variety of small-scale family businesses such as street vending, hawking, and crafts. For years these "informal sectors" were ignored by governments. They were thought to weaken the economy by not paying taxes, undermining city services, and aggravating urban environmental problems. As the sheer size and vigor of these settlements have become apparent, planners have begun to take them more seriously, and to appreciate the contribution made toward such things as water vending, recycling of scrap, informal markets, jewelry and crafting, tailoring, repair services, and other small self-employed businesses.

What the colors and symbols mean

Number of people per square mile

25 to 50   Uninhabited land   2 to 25

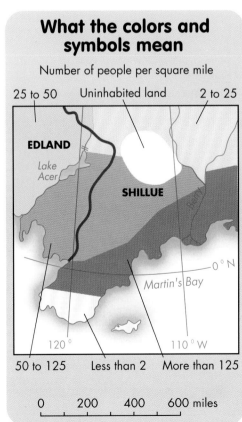

EDLAND

Lake Acer

SHILLUE

0°N

Martin's Bay

120°   110°W

50 to 125   Less than 2   More than 125

0   200   400   600 miles

Uninhabited except for research scientists and other workers, Antarctica is generally ownerless. International agreements on scientific investigation allow many different nationalities to work here.

Human Races

The number of human races varies according to the purposes of the classification. At one time there were thought to be just three different races — Caucasoid, Mongoloid, and Negroid. Scientific study has shown this to be an inaccurate and oversimplified classification. Today many geographical races are recognized, and even more local races.

The principal geographical races are:

African — also known as Negroid. A collection of related races originating south of the Sahara. Members have curly or tightly coiled hair, thick lips, and large amounts of melanin in their skin, hair, and gums. These people have genetically adapted to cope with diseases such as malaria. Most American blacks are of African origin.

American Indian — sometimes called Amerindian. This race is related to the Asian geographical race but differs in various blood group frequencies. For thousands of years the American Indians were the only people in the western hemisphere. Their skin varies from dark to light brown, and they have straight dark hair.

African Bushman

Chinese woman

Asian — also called Mongoloid. This group includes populations all of continental Asia except for South Asia and the Middle East. It extends to Japan, the Philippin and most of Indonesia. Member have straight hair, inner eyefolds and pads of fat over their cheekbones. They have light bro skin, and most are of shorter stature than Caucasians.

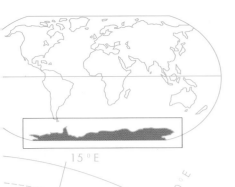

Australian — or Australian Aborigine, or Australoid. A distinct group of races, members of which have large teeth, moderate to heavy skin coloring, narrow skulls, and a moderate amount of body hair.

European — sometimes called Caucasoid. Includes populations of Europe, the Middle East, and Africa north of the Sahara. Members have lighter skins than people from other geographical races, though in the southern areas many have dark skins.

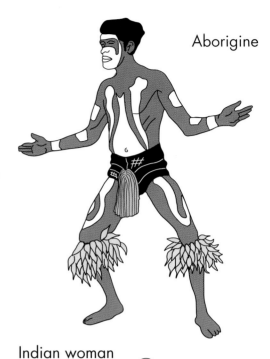

Aborigine

Indian woman

Indian — includes people of South Asia, and extends from the Himalayas to the Indian Ocean. Skin color ranges from light in the north to dark in the south.

Polynesian man

Micronesian — peoples who occupy a series of Pacific Islands, including the Gilberts. Members are dark-skinned and small, with wavy or wooly hair.

Polynesian — a group of Pacific Island peoples living from New Zealand to Hawaii. Members are tall and often stout, with light to moderate skin color.

anesian — the Melanesian and
ıan group includes the dark-
ned people of New Guinea and
Solomon Islands. They
mble Africans in skin color but
n blood group.

The unique age distribution pattern of China is the result of a deliberate policy to bring births and deaths into balance in a short period of time. This decision will have significant consequences for the future of the country.

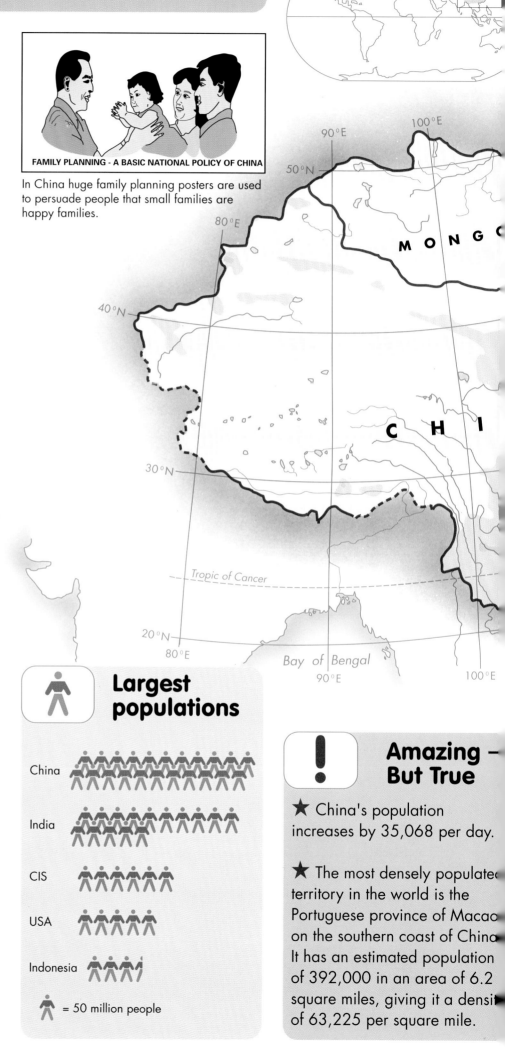

FAMILY PLANNING - A BASIC NATIONAL POLICY OF CHINA

In China huge family planning posters are used to persuade people that small families are happy families.

China

China has a unique age distribution pattern, brought about because of an enormous change in both births and deaths over a short time. First there was a dramatic decrease in mortality, followed immediately by a policy of forced birth control that allowed only one child per couple.

China's initially high birth rate in 1950–55 was 44 births per thousand of population. This dropped moderately to 31 by 1970–75, but during this period the death rate dropped dramatically from 25 to 9 per thousand. The rate of natural increase rose from 1.9 to 2.2 per cent between 1950 and 1975.

Children under 4 years old had traditionally had a high death rate, but with major improvements in health, sanitation, education, and medical conditions, child mortality rates fell dramatically from 266 per thousand births to 83. Today, people born between 1965 and 1970 comprise the single largest population group in China.

With the "one child per family" policy in the late 1970s, many changes started to occur. The number of children born between 1975 and 1980 fell steeply to 98 million. Although this policy has now been relaxed, the birth rate has continued to remain low.

Largest populations

China
India
CIS
USA
Indonesia

= 50 million people

Amazing – But True

★ China's population increases by 35,068 per day.

★ The most densely populated territory in the world is the Portuguese province of Macao on the southern coast of China. It has an estimated population of 392,000 in an area of 6.2 square miles, giving it a density of 63,225 per square mile.

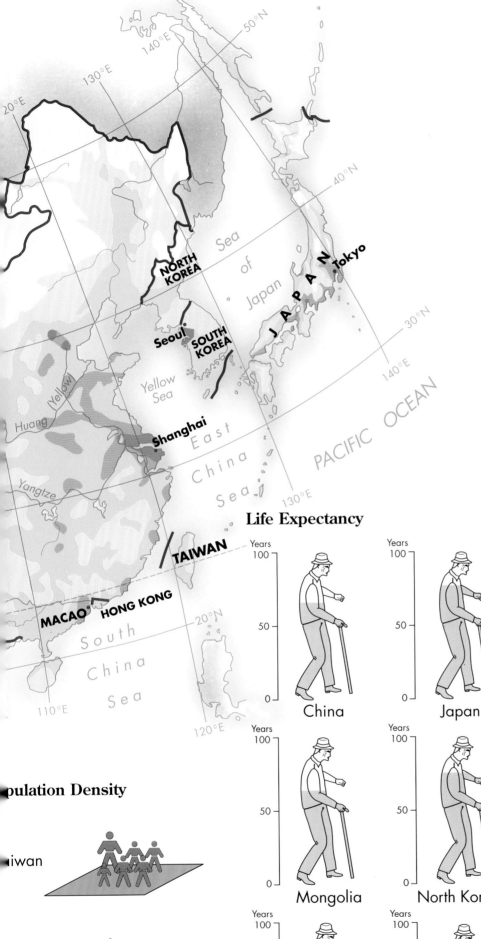

NORTH KOREA
Seoul SOUTH KOREA
Sea of Japan
J A P A N Tokyo
Yellow Sea
Huang (Yellow)
Yangtze
Shanghai
East China Sea
PACIFIC OCEAN
TAIWAN
MACAO HONG KONG
South China Sea

Fewest dentists

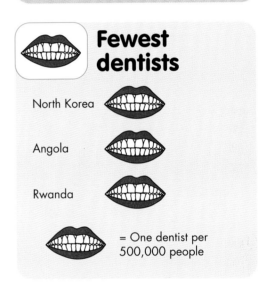

North Korea

Angola

Rwanda

= One dentist per 500,000 people

Life Expectancy

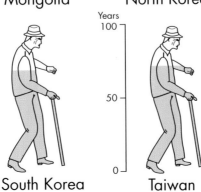

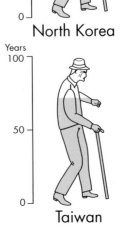

Years	
100	100
50	50
0	0
China	Japan

Years	
100	100
50	50
0	0
Mongolia	North Korea

Years	
100	100
50	50
0	0
South Korea	Taiwan

What the colors and symbols mean

Number of people per square mile

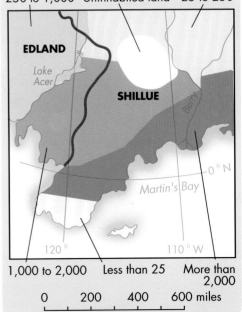

250 to 1,000   Uninhabited land   25 to 250

EDLAND
Lake Acer
SHILLUE
Martin's Bay

1,000 to 2,000   Less than 25   More than 2,000

| 0 | 200 | 400 | 600 miles |

Population Density

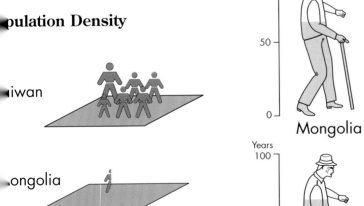

Taiwan

Mongolia

Number of people per square mile

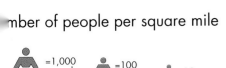

= 1,000 people   = 100 people   = 10 people

Some of the most densely populated countries of the world are found in Asia. Both Europe and Asia have close to 265 people per square mile, but this figure on its own tells nothing about the quality of life.

Population Density

Population density is the total population of the country divided by its area — usually expressed as number of people per square mile. To some extent, population density is an indication of prosperity because a high level of urbanization usually goes with a high population density. The most densely populated countries are the "city - states" like Singapore, but highly urbanized countries such as Japan, Netherlands, and the UK are also high on the list. The most crowded country, excluding the city - states, is Bangladesh, where the high fertility of the land supports a dense rural population.

Countries with the lowest population densities usually have a high proportion of almost uninhabitable land, such as the deserts in Namibia and Mongolia.

Population Density

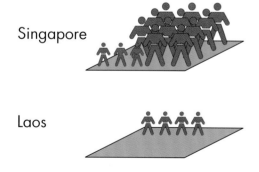

Singapore

Laos

Number of people per square mile

 =1,000 people =100 people =10 people

Life Expectancy

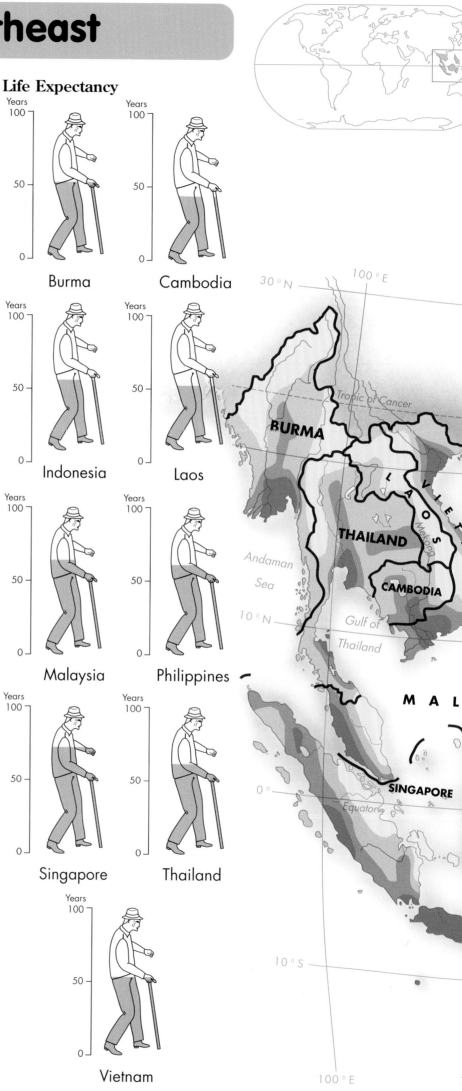

Burma

Cambodia

Indonesia

Laos

Malaysia

Philippines

Singapore

Thailand

Vietnam

Amazing – But True

It took thousands of years for e human population to reach a lion and then only 100 years r it to double to 2 billion.

Safe Drinking Water

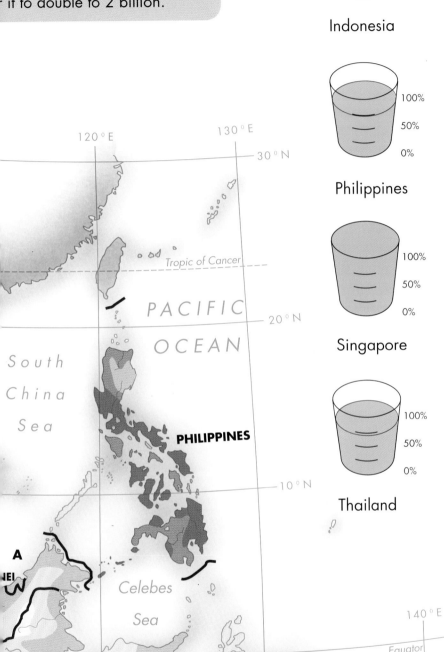

100%
50%
0%

Indonesia

100%
50%
0%

Philippines

100%
50%
0%

Singapore

100%
50%
0%

Thailand

Singapore

Singapore has one of the highest population densities in the world, and it has had one of the most successful family planning programs. It dates back to 1949, when a voluntary organization was set up to provide health care for children and mothers and to advise on birth control. In 1966 it was superseded by a government organization. Both abortion and sterilization are legal, and there are a large number of penalties for having large families. Posters actively promote two–child families, and radio, television, schools and exhibitions are used to get the message across. The average age of marriage is high. This helps to reduce the number of births.

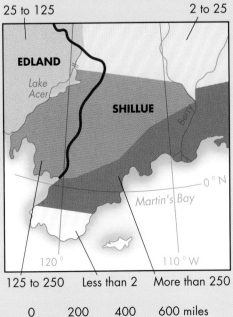

What the colors and symbols mean

Number of people per square mile

25 to 125   2 to 25

EDLAND

Lake Acer

SHILLUE

Martin's Bay

125 to 250   Less than 2   More than 250

0   200   400   600 miles

The population structure of the more developed regions is generally more balanced. It is a result of a steady decline in the death rate, producing an older population, along with a falling birthrate.

The More Developed Regions

The more developed regions, as defined by the United Nations, include the United States, Canada, Japan, Europe, Australia, New Zealand, and the former Soviet Union. These countries share a population pattern that is quite different from Africa's. It is a better–balanced pattern of age distribution. It reflects the trend of low and falling birth rates and low death rates that have produced an older and aging population.

The numbers of those over 65 and those under 15 will be almost equal by the year 2025. By then the older part of the population will make up 19% and the younger 18% of the total.

Population Density

New Zealand

Australia

Number of people per square mi

= 1,000 people	= 100 people	= 10 peop

What the colors and symbols mean

Number of people per square mile

25 to 50	Uninhabited land	2 to 25

EDLAND

Lake Acer

SHILLUE

Belly

0° N

Martin's Bay

120°

110° W

50 to 125	Less than 2	More than 125

0   200   400   600 miles

Life Expectancy

Years
100

50

0

Australia

Years
100

50

0

New Zealand

Years
100

50

0

Papua New
Guinea

Cities over 5 million

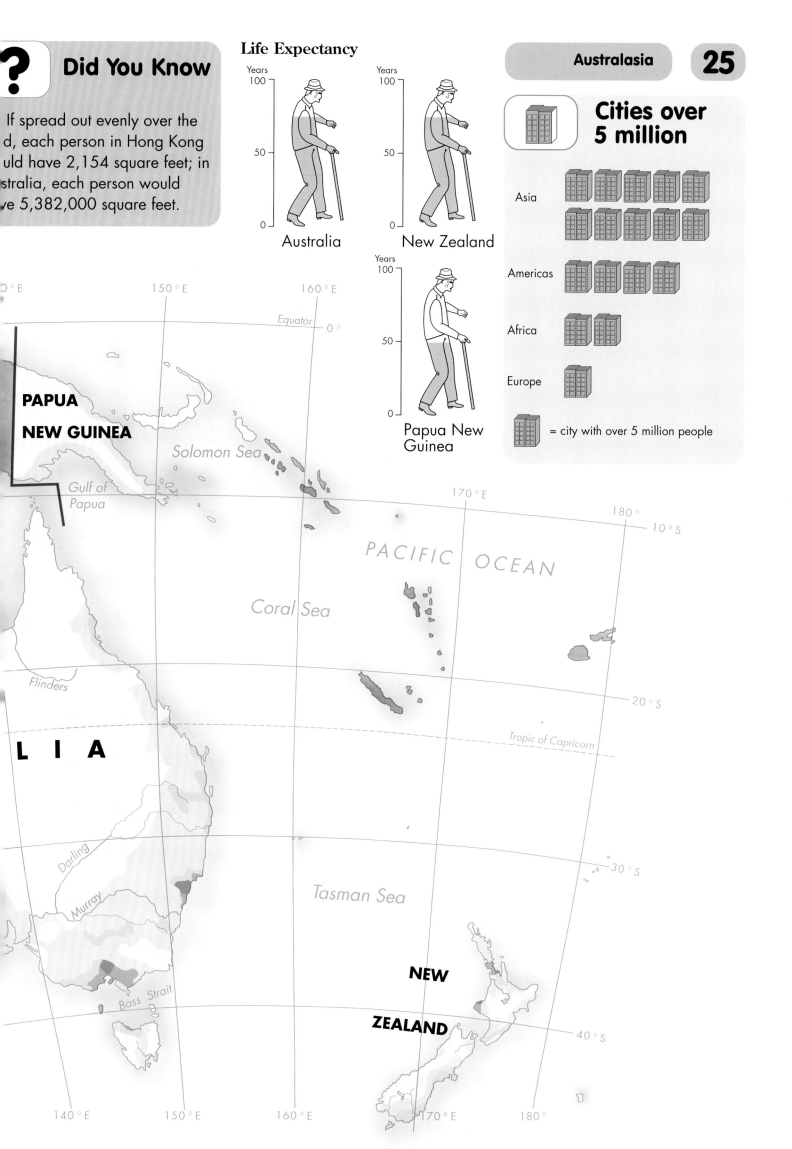

Asia

Americas

Africa

Europe

= city with over 5 million people

150°E

160°E

Equator 0°

PAPUA

NEW GUINEA

Solomon Sea

Gulf of
Papua

170°E

180°

10°S

PACIFIC OCEAN

Coral Sea

20°S

Flinders

Tropic of Capricorn

L I A

30°S

Darling

Tasman Sea

Murray

NEW

Bass Strait

ZEALAND

40°S

140°E

150°E

160°E

170°E

180°

Health and education seem to be two of the most important factors in reducing birth rates. Family planning policies that have ignored social conditions and poverty have rarely been successful.

Family Planning

Fifty years ago giving information on birth control was illegal in the US, and the population explosion was not thought to be a problem. Today birth control facilities are present in nearly every country, and most governments have population programs.

According to the International Planned Parenthood Federation, some 400 million couples of reproductive age in developing countries are not practicing contraception. The forces working against cutting fertility rates are heavily based in social, cultural, and economic conditions. Fertility rates are highest in countries where there is economic deprivation and lowest in affluent societies. Some of the reasons for wanting a large family include high infant mortality, labor–intensive means of subsistence, and the need for support in old age.

Better health, better employment prospects, better education, and a secure old age result in cuts in the fertility rate. But these trends are hard to influence. Often it is the very lack of birth control that makes these things so hard to achieve.

Population Density

Canada

Number of people per square mile

 =1,000 people   =100 people   =10 people

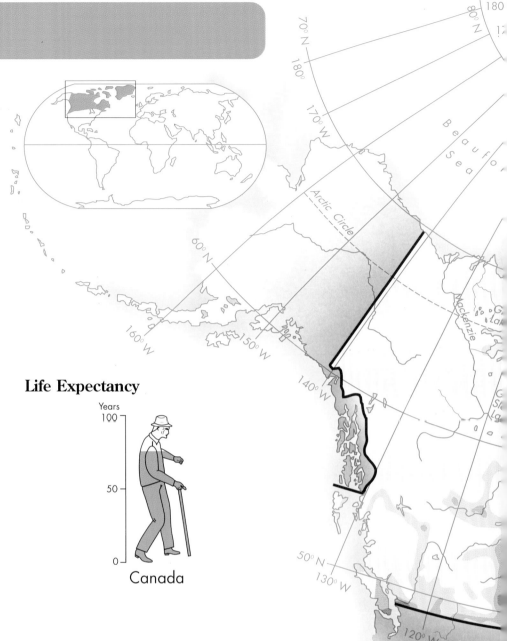

Life Expectancy

Canada

What the colors and symbols mean

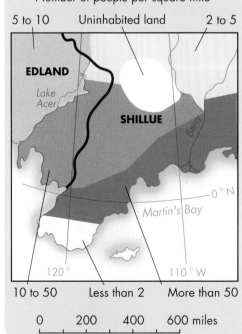

Number of people per square mile

| 5 to 10 | Uninhabited land | 2 to 5 |
| 10 to 50 | Less than 2 | More than 50 |

EDLAND

Lake Acer

SHILLUE

Martin's Bay

0 200 400 600 miles

Examples of Family Planning

West Germany

West Germany has the lowest population growth in the world, if its population rate continues to decline as it is there will be one retired person for each person in work by 2050. The burden for the social services is potentially huge. West Germany is actually trying encourage births.

China

With 23% of the world's population but only 7% of its land, China face huge potential problem. In 1978 Chinese policy makers set a target of 1.2 billion people for the year 2000. To achieve this they implemented a controversial

ARCTIC
OCEAN

Greenland

Baffin Bay

Davis Strait

Labrador Sea

Hudson Bay

Nelson

C A N A D A

Lake Manitoba *Lake Winnipeg*

ATLANTIC OCEAN

Lake Superior

Lake Michigan *Lake Huron* *Lake Erie* *Lake Ontario*

Amazing – But True

★ Greenland is the most sparsely inhabited territory apart from Antarctica. With a population of 53,406 in an area of 840,000 square miles, there is about one person for every 15.7 square miles. However, about 83% of the island is an uninhabitable ice cap.

-child, one–couple policy. Using ial propaganda, peer and group sure, and extensive education, launched the strictest birth rol program in history. Couples conceived second children e encouraged to seek an tion. If they produced the child were forced to pay back fits and pay fines. The number erilizations soared, reaching ly 8.86 million in 1984. e then the policy has been ed. Research has revealed that -children families are ptable. But the one–child policy ll encouraged, and the birth has remained low.

Family Planning

Space your children better your life

Family Planning poster in Kenya

Zaire

Zaire suffers from high fertility as well as from high infant mortality and maternal mortality rates. Contraception is practiced by as few as 2% of the population, and there is an enormous need for family planning services. In 1982 an experimental community–based health policy was initiated, based around traditional birth attendants. These were local women, often largely illiterate, who were trusted and experienced midwives. These women have been educated and trained in modern techniques of maternity care and family planning. The community finances the training. Local health centers have been established. Since the program was started, an increasing number of women have been attending clinics, and there has been a drop in infant and child deaths.

Increasing food production to feed a growing population is not the only consideration; making sure food reaches the population at reasonably affordable prices may in itself be a difficult task. Failure to feed a hungry population often leads to civil unrest.

World Health Organization

WHO is a special agency of the United Nations which helps build better health systems throughout the world, especially in developing countries.

Prevention of disease is important. WHO works with governments to provide safe drinking water, adequate sewage disposal, and immunization against childhood diseases. WHO helps to identify important research goals in the fields of diseases, food and nutrition, and biological and pharmaceutical research. WHO's headquarters is in Geneva, Switzerland.

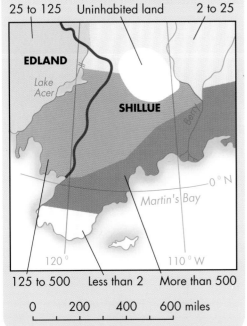

What the colors and symbols mean

Number of people per square mile

25 to 125   Uninhabited land   2 to 25

EDLAND
Lake Acer
SHILLUE
Martin's Bay

125 to 500   Less than 2   More than 500

0   200   400   600 miles

Population Density

Armenia

Azerbaijan

Belarus

Estonia

Georgia

Kazakhstan

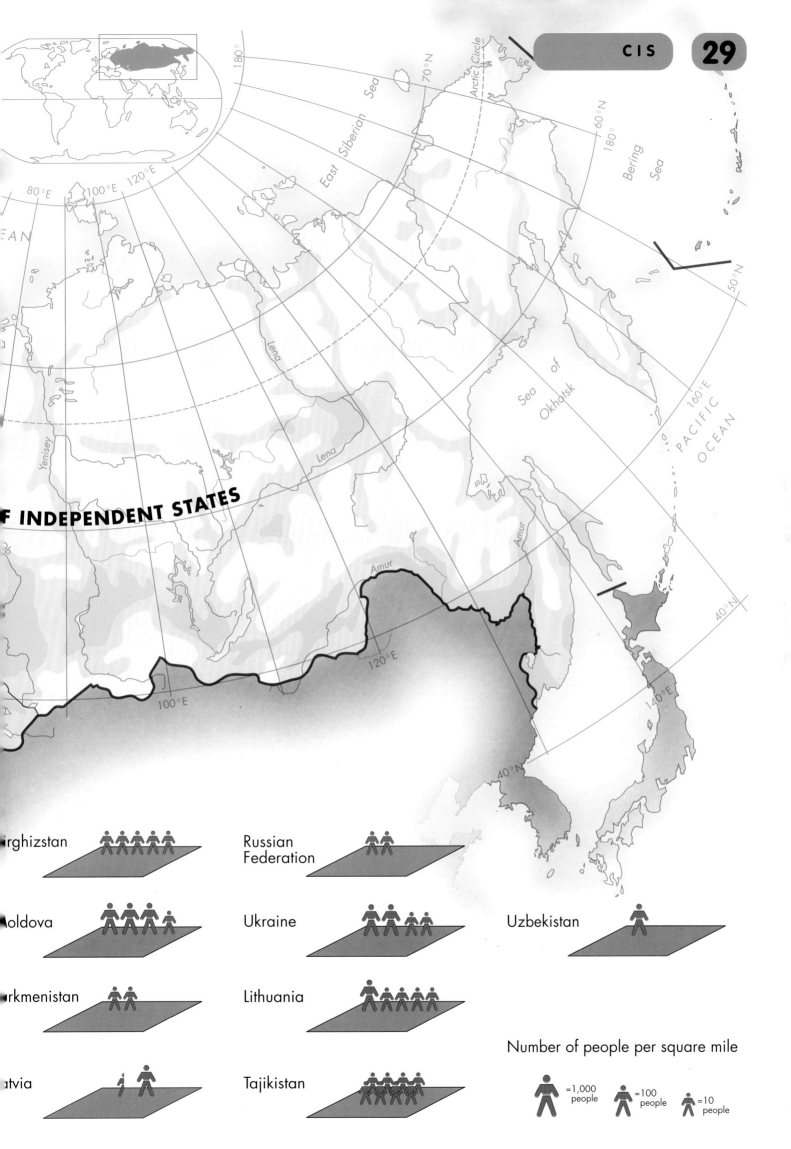

F INDEPENDENT STATES

Number of people per square mile

rghizstan

Russian Federation

oldova

Ukraine

Uzbekistan

rkmenistan

Lithuania

tvia

Tajikistan

= 1,000 people

= 100 people

= 10 people

One-third of the world's people are ill at any one time, and most of them are in developing countries. Wealth promotes health and health in turn promotes wealth. The sick and weak remain poor.

Health

Generally, as a country becomes richer it spends more on health. Spending on health as a percentage of GNP has risen steadily in developed countries.
In fact, health spending has risen so sharply over the last 30 years, partly because of the escalating cost of new technologies, that many countries are concerned at the cost. They began to cut back on public spending in the 1980s and to emphasize private medical care.

It is the degree of private spending on health that varies most within the developed nations. Denmark and the UK, where public health care is generally "free at the point of use," use relatively little private money and so spend a smaller proportion of their GDP on health than countries of similar wealth. The US spends the greatest proportion of GDP, though it does not necessarily achieve a higher standard of public health care.

Poorer countries lack medical resources and skills. This is one of the main reasons for high mortality rates. The imbalance is noticeable for doctors and even worse for dentists.

Population Density

Malta

Number of people per square mile

= 1,000 people
= 100 people
= 10 people

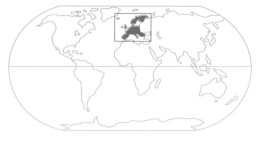

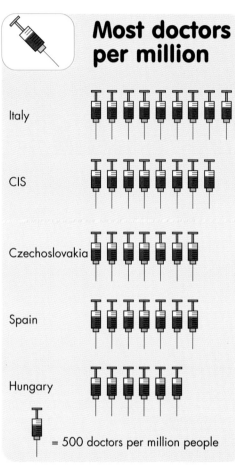

Most doctors per million

- Italy
- CIS
- Czechoslovakia
- Spain
- Hungary

= 500 doctors per million people

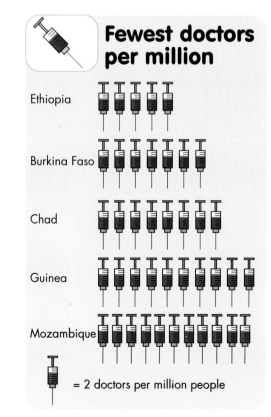

Fewest doctors per million

- Ethiopia
- Burkina Faso
- Chad
- Guinea
- Mozambique

= 2 doctors per million people

Most hospital beds per person

- Finland
- Sweden
- France
- Netherlands
- Japan

= 10 people per bed

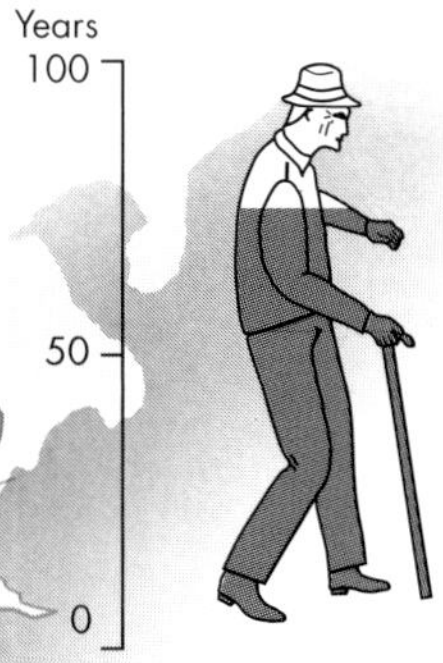

Life Expectancy

Albania

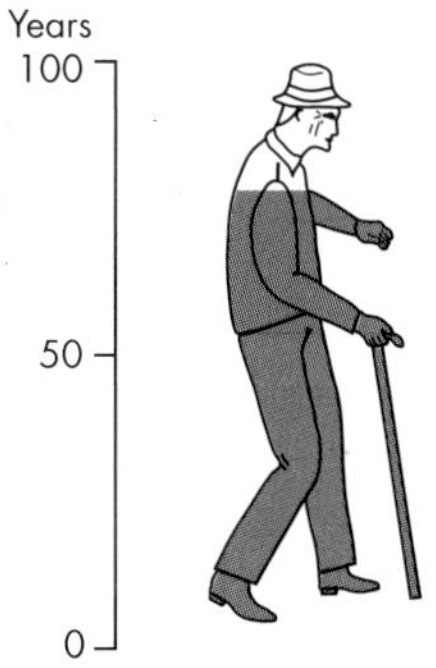

Bulgaria

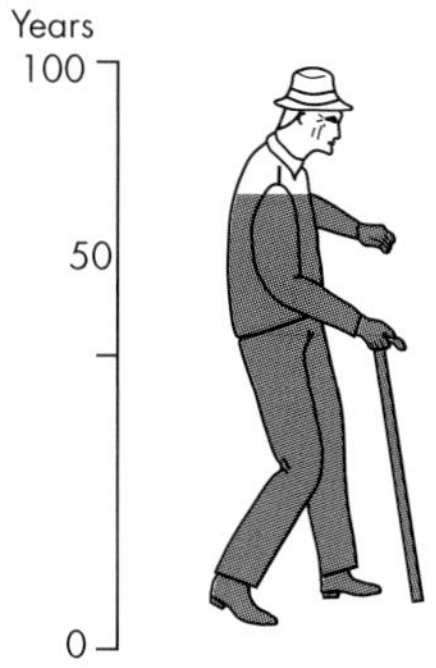

Cyprus

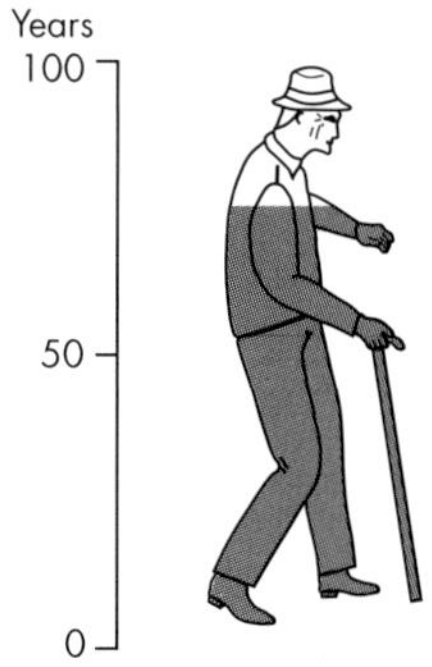

Czechoslovakia

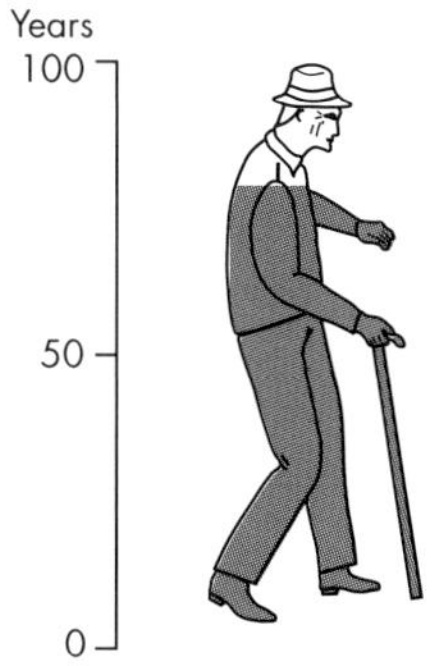

Finland

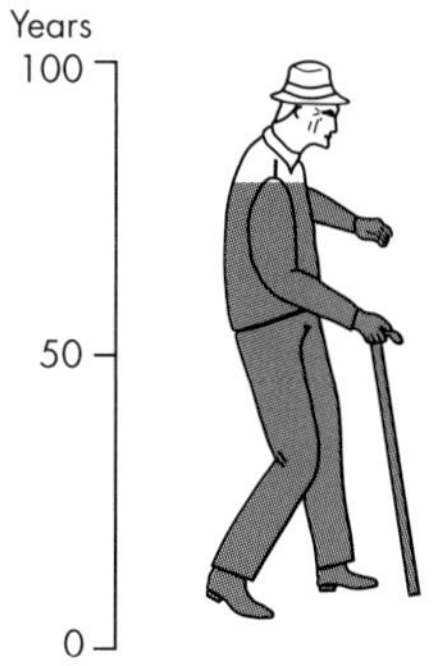

Greece

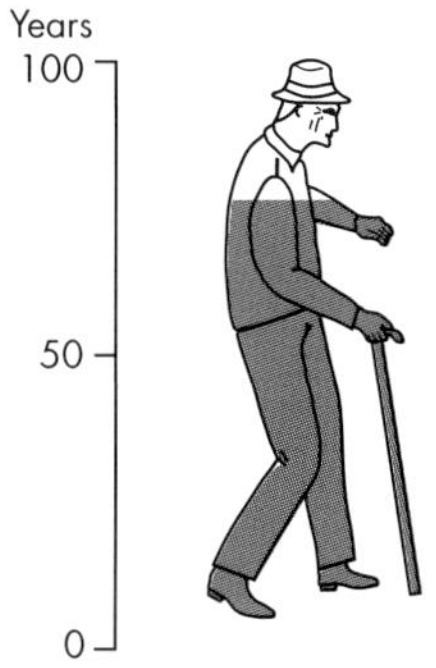

Hungary

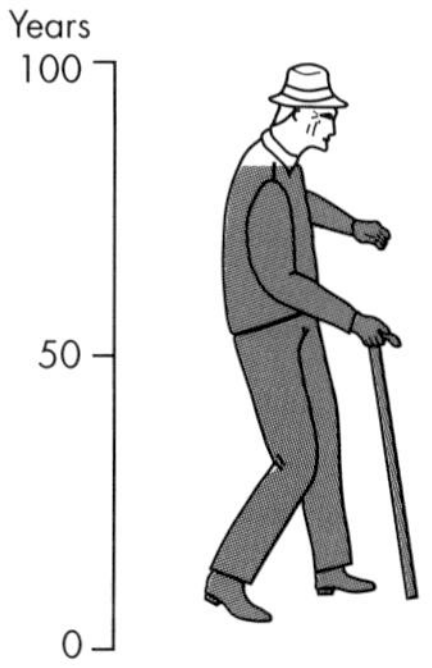

Iceland

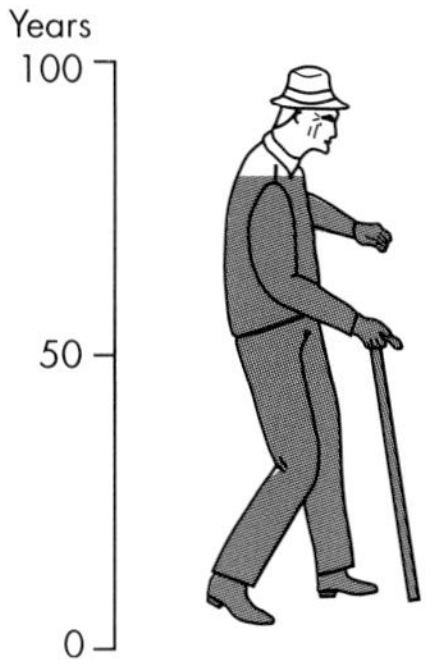

Norway

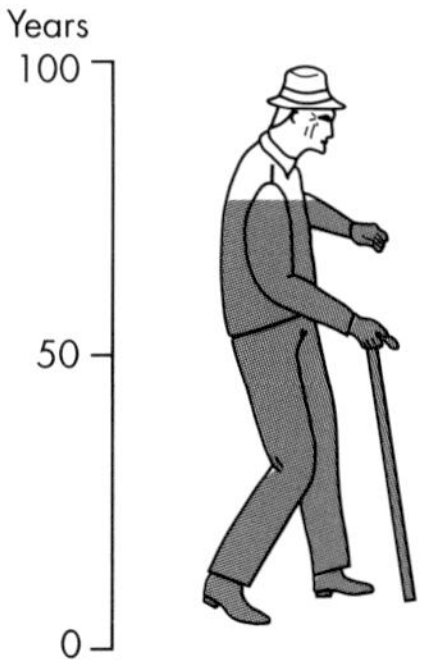

Poland

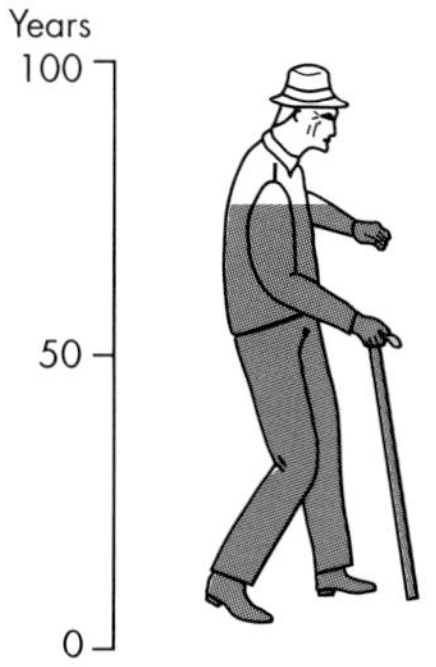

Romania

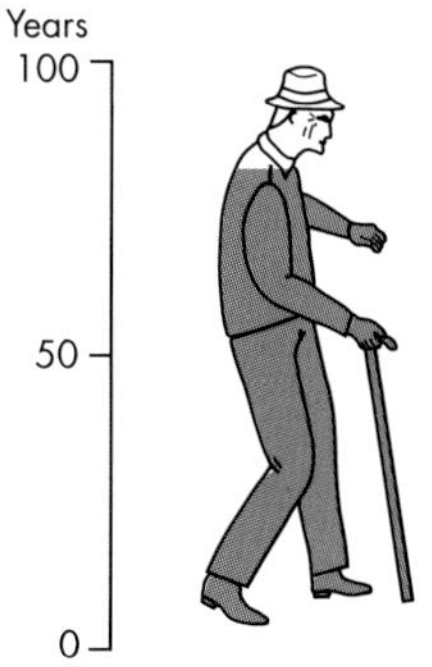

Sweden

What the colors and symbols mean

Number of people per square mile

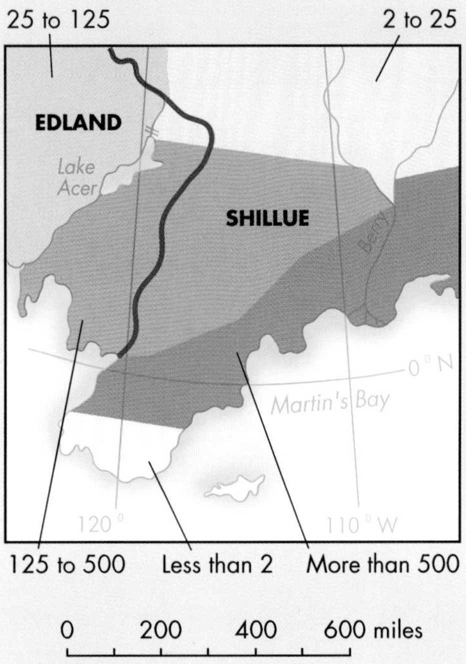

25 to 125   2 to 25

EDLAND

Lake Acer

SHILLUE

Martin's Bay

120°   110°W

125 to 500   Less than 2   More than 500

0   200   400   600 miles

? Did You Know

The Vatican City has no births
because no married people live
here.

The principality of Monaco
on the south coast of France has
a population of 27,000 in an
area of 473 acres, a density
equal to 38,179 people per
square mile.

Age structure in the population indicates future trends that have important implications for management of resources, and for economic and social development. An increasingly elderly population in Europe will create many new problems.

Future Lifestyles

It is hard to understand how the social and demographic changes that are taking place now will affect future lifestyles. There is a great contrast between what will happen in the developed and the developing parts of the world. In the developed countries the population will become increasingly elderly, and the work force will shrink. Along with the technological revolution this may mean a great many people do not work. Formal employment may take a lesser role in most people's lives. Education in self–employment and leisure skills will become a priority. Cities may well decline, and ethnic minorities will grow.

With a much smaller work force generating income, there may be difficulties in supporting the workless and in finding the health and social services necessary for the elderly. A growing underclass of poor already exists. In the USA, the added influx of minorities could lead to a poor majority.

Life in poor countries in Africa can be grim. Funding from outside is necessary to develop education, health, industry, and sustainable agriculture. High birth rates and an overstretched agricultural economy lead to disaster.

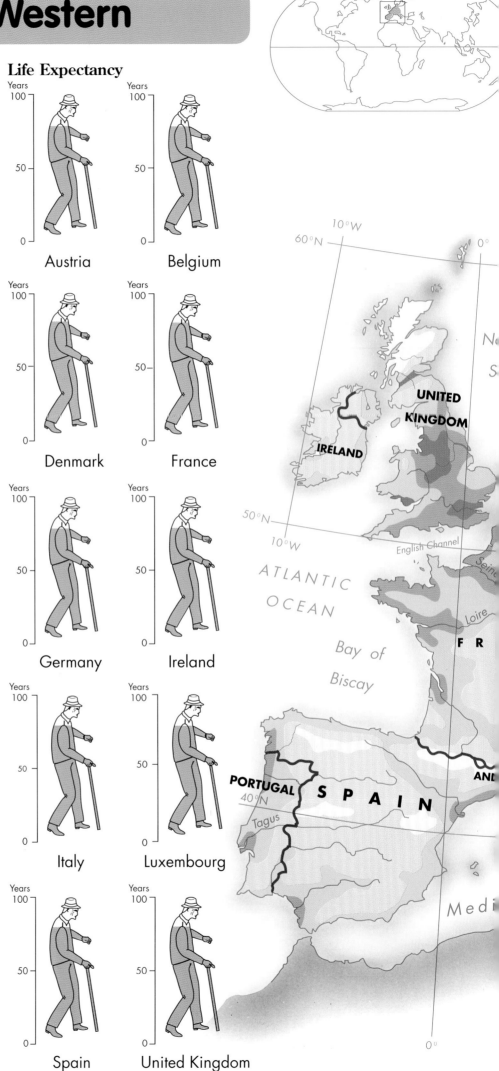

Life Expectancy

Austria

Belgium

Denmark

France

Germany

Ireland

Italy

Luxembourg

Spain

United Kingdom

Population Density

Belgium

UK

Number of people per square mile

👤 = 1,000 people   👤 = 100 people   👤 = 10 people

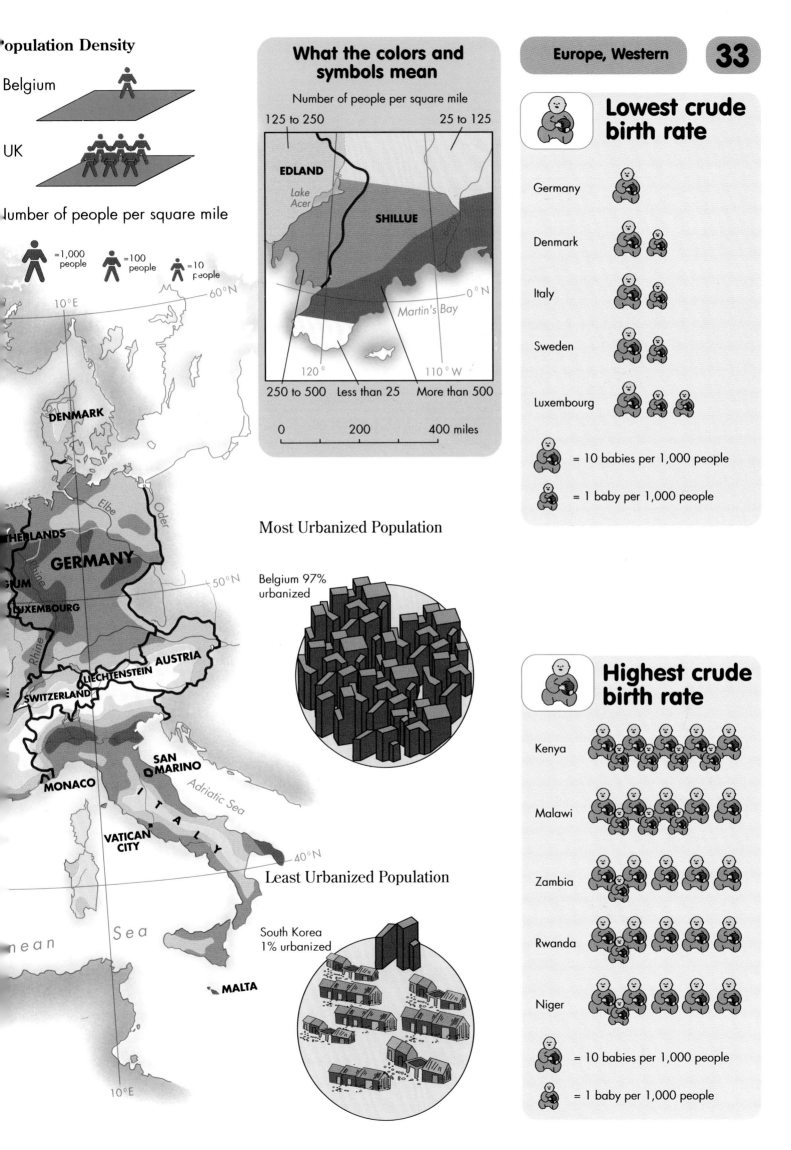

DENMARK

NETHERLANDS

GERMANY

Elbe

Oder

BELGIUM

LUXEMBOURG

Rhine

SWITZERLAND

LIECHTENSTEIN

AUSTRIA

MONACO

SAN MARINO

I T A L Y

Adriatic Sea

VATICAN CITY

MALTA

Sea

nean

10°E

60°N

50°N

40°N

10°E

What the colors and symbols mean

Number of people per square mile

125 to 250   25 to 125

EDLAND

Lake Acer

SHILLUE

Martin's Bay

0°N

120°   110° W

250 to 500   Less than 25   More than 500

0   200   400 miles

Lowest crude birth rate

Germany

Denmark

Italy

Sweden

Luxembourg

👶 = 10 babies per 1,000 people

👶 = 1 baby per 1,000 people

Most Urbanized Population

Belgium 97% urbanized

Least Urbanized Population

South Korea 1% urbanized

Highest crude birth rate

Kenya

Malawi

Zambia

Rwanda

Niger

👶 = 10 babies per 1,000 people

👶 = 1 baby per 1,000 people

Unclean drinking water is one of the leading causes of death in the developing countries. In India three young children die every minute from drinking dirty water.

Water and Sanitation

Rapid population growth means pressure on sanitation, water, and energy resources. Population growth also places rising pollution pressure on rivers.

In most Third World countries, the effort to deliver water supplies to new neighborhoods has outweighed the commitment to treat and dispose of waste. In these areas, rivers, estuaries, and coastal zones are badly polluted by sewage. Groundwater resources are threatened by uncontrolled dump sites. Studies of 24 rivers in Central and South America found more than half of them severely polluted by sewage.

There is a growing realization that poor sanitation and lack of investment in sewage treatment takes a heavy toll on human health and living conditions.

In 1985, 75% of the urban inhabitants in developing countries had access to safe drinking water, and 59% had access to sanitation services. But these figures may not be as good as they appear. The World Health Organization (WHO) defines access to safe drinking water as access to piped water or a public standpipe within 219 yards of a dwelling. Access to sanitation is defined as waste disposal by way of public sewers, pit latrines, pour–flush lavatories, septic tanks, or communal toilets. WHO estimates that only 12% of urban dwellers in Africa were served by sewer connections.

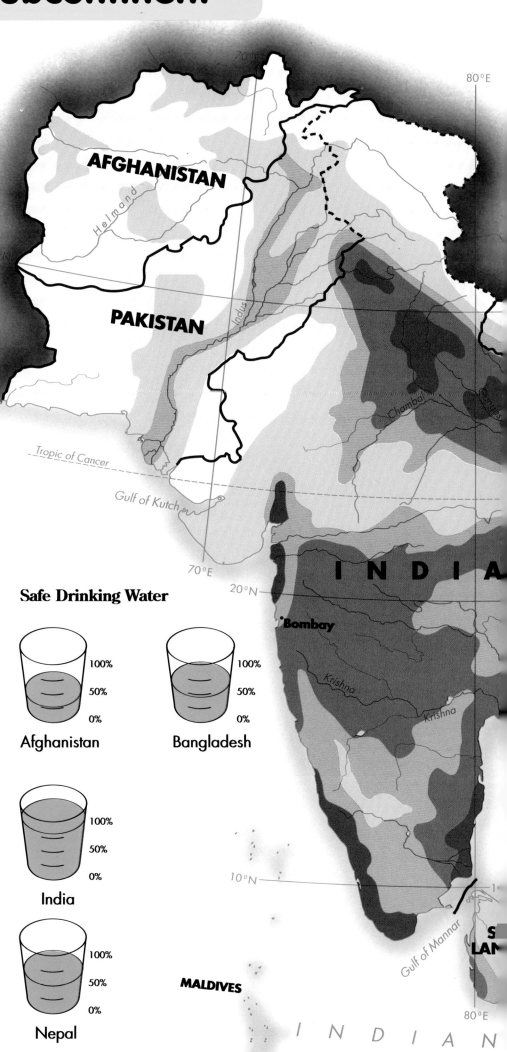

Safe Drinking Water

Afghanistan

Bangladesh

India

Nepal

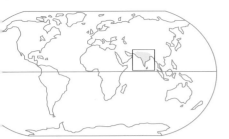

Life Expectancy

Years
100

50

0

Afghanistan

Years
100

50

0

Bangladesh

Years
100

50

0

India

Years
100

50

0

Nepal

Years
100

50

0

Sri Lanka

Did You Know

The lowest recorded
[ex]pectation for life is recorded in
[Af]ghanistan as 36.6 years for
[ma]les and 37.3 years for
[fem]ales.

30°N

BHUTAN

Brahmaputra

BANGLADESH

Tropic of Cancer

Calcutta

20°N

90°E

*Bay of
Bengal*

[Pop]ulation Density

[Af]ghanistan

[Ba]ngladesh

[Num]ber of people per square mile

 =1,000 people   =100 people   =10 people

*Andaman
Sea*

[O]CEAN

Most child deaths

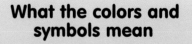

Afghanistan

Mali

Sierra Leone

Malawi

Ethiopia

= 50 per 1,000   = 10 per 1,000

What the colors and symbols mean

Number of people per square mile

125 to 250   Uninhabited land   25 to 125

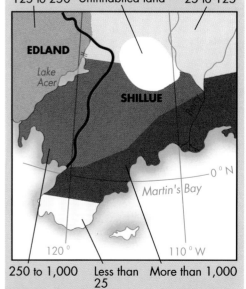

EDLAND

*Lake
Acer*

SHILLUE

0°N

Martin's Bay

120°   110°W

250 to 1,000   Less than 25   More than 1,000

0   200   400 miles

Drought and desertification have driven millions of people off the land in the early 1980s. The number of environmental refugees will grow with the warming of the world climate and the overuse of land.

Refugees

A person forced to flee his or her country of origin and seek safety elsewhere is known as a refugee, or displaced person. Most refugees flee to escape persecution because of race, religion, nationality, or political beliefs.

Wars and revolutions continue to create large numbers of refugees. Since the Communists took over in 1975, 1.5 million people have fled from Cambodia, Laos, and Vietnam. Others have fled from Bangladesh, China, Eastern Europe, and Palestine. In the 1980s there were refugees from Afghanistan, Cambodia, Vietnam, Eastern Africa, Central America, and Eastern Europe.

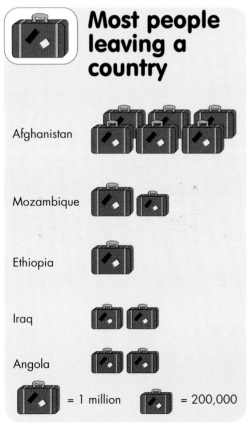

Most people leaving a country

Afghanistan	
Mozambique	
Ethiopia	
Iraq	
Angola	

= 1 million   = 200,000

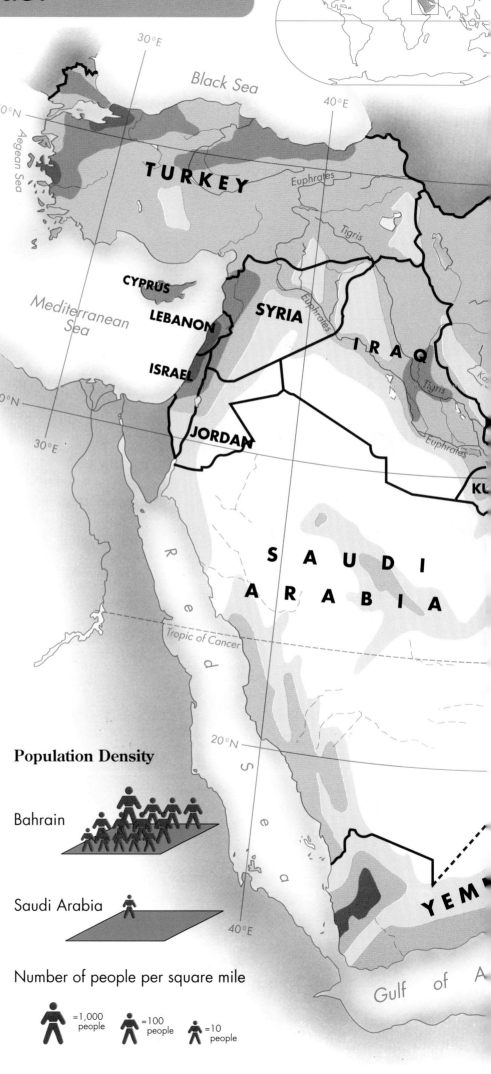

Population Density

Bahrain

Saudi Arabia

Number of people per square mile

= 1,000 people   = 100 people   = 10 people

Foreign born populations

United Arab Emirates	3.5 figures
Israel	2.5 figures
Kuwait	2.5 figures
Bahrain	1.5 figures
Ivory Coast	1 figure

👤 = 20% of total population

Life Expectancy

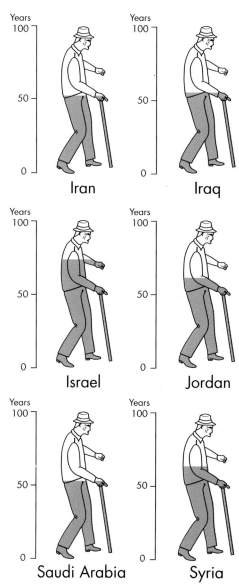

Iran   Iraq

Israel   Jordan

Saudi Arabia   Syria

Homes for refugees

Pakistan	🧳🧳🧳🧳🧳🧳🧳
Iran	🧳🧳🧳🧳
Jordan	🧳🧳🧳🧳🧳
Israel	🧳🧳🧳🧳
Ethiopia	🧳🧳🧳

🧳 = 1 million   🧳 = 200,000

What the colors and symbols mean

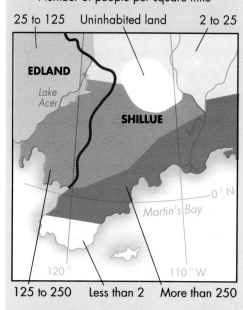

Number of people per square mile

25 to 125   Uninhabited land   2 to 25

EDLAND
Lake Acer
SHILLUE
Martin's Bay

120°   110°W

125 to 250   Less than 2   More than 250

0   200   400 miles

I R A N

Gulf
Gulf of Oman
Tropic of Cancer

UNITED ARAB EMIRATES

OMAN

BAHRAIN
QATAR

Arabian Sea

60°E
40°N
30°N
20°N

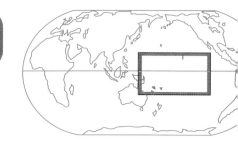

Increases in life expectancy mean that children in Oceania can expect to live 4.9 more years than they would have 20 years ago. The birth rate is still very high in many of the island communities.

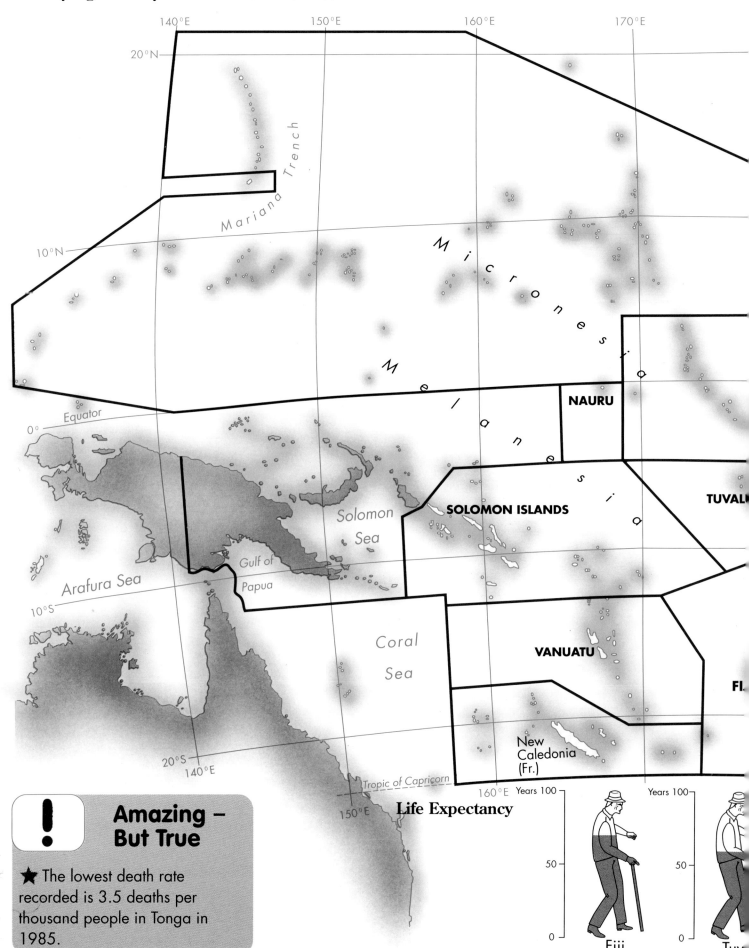

140°E
150°E
160°E
170°E
20°N
Mariana Trench
10°N
Micronesia
Melanesia
Equator
0°
NAURU
SOLOMON ISLANDS
TUVAL
Solomon Sea
Gulf of Papua
Arafura Sea
10°S
Coral Sea
VANUATU
FI.
New Caledonia (Fr.)
20°S
140°E
Tropic of Capricorn
150°E
160°E
Life Expectancy
Years 100
Years 100
50
50
0
Fiji
0
Tuv

Amazing – But True

★ The lowest death rate recorded is 3.5 deaths per thousand people in Tonga in 1985.

What the colors and symbols mean

Number of people per square mile

EDLAND

Lake Acer

SHILLUE

Berry

0° N

Martin's Bay

120°

110° W

Less than 1

| 0 | 200 | 400 | 600 miles |

Population Density

Fiji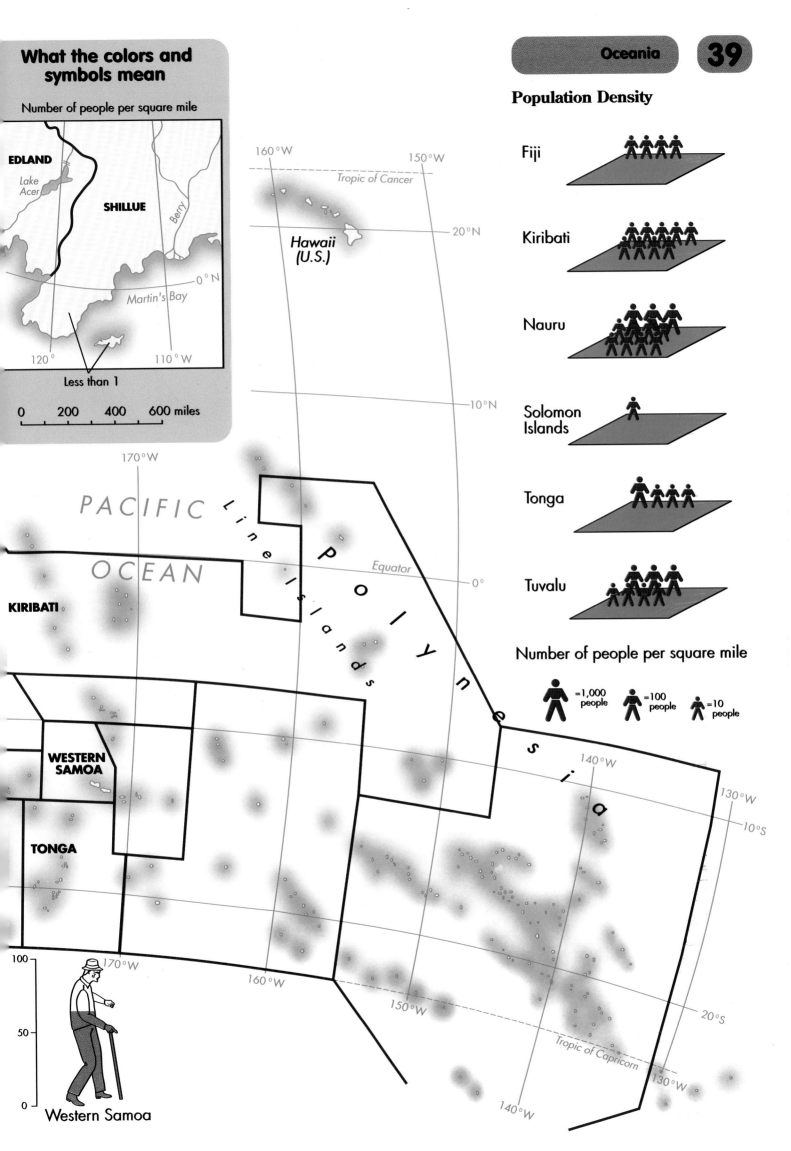

Kiribati

Nauru

Solomon Islands

Tonga

Tuvalu

Number of people per square mile

= 1,000 people   = 100 people   = 10 people

160°W

Tropic of Cancer

150°W

20°N

Hawaii (U.S.)

10°N

170°W

PACIFIC

Line Islands

OCEAN

P O l y n e s i a

Equator

0°

KIRIBATI

140°W

130°W

10°S

WESTERN SAMOA

TONGA

100

170°W

160°W

150°W

20°S

Tropic of Capricorn

130°W

140°W

50

0

Western Samoa

The death toll from AIDS may not be huge compared with other major world diseases, but it is particularly worrying because it tends to kill young and middle-aged adults in their most productive years.

World Disease

Far more money is invested in curing diseases than in preventing them, though most of the world's premature deaths occur as a result of poverty, contaminated water, lack of proper sanitation, and poor medical facilities. These problems have on the whole been eliminated from developed countries; the people of Northern Europe, North America, Australia, and Japan tend to die of diseases of old age and abundance, while in Africa, South America, and Asia they die of diseases of deprivation.

In developed countries about half of all deaths are caused by coronary heart disease and cerebrovascular disease, associated with a rich diet high in animal fats, lack of exercise, and tobacco.

Another contributing factor, though hard to quantify, is stress. Expenditure on tranquilizers in Europe and North America exceeds the entire budget of the world's 60 poorest countries. Drug addiction and alcoholism are signs of stress, as is the exceedingly high suicide rate.

By contrast, in the developing countries, deaths from cancer and cardiovascular diseases combined make up only a quarter of the total deaths, due partly to low life expectancy. Diarrhea and associated infections are major killers here. The victims are mainly children under the age of five years.

Measles, whooping cough, polio, tuberculosis, tetanus, and diptheria are major child-killers, accounting for more than 5 million deaths worldwide each year. Immunization is possible against all these diseases. Almost all the deaths occur in Third World countries, where many children are not vaccinated. In Ethiopia, for example, only about 16% of children are vaccinated, even fewer in Bangladesh.

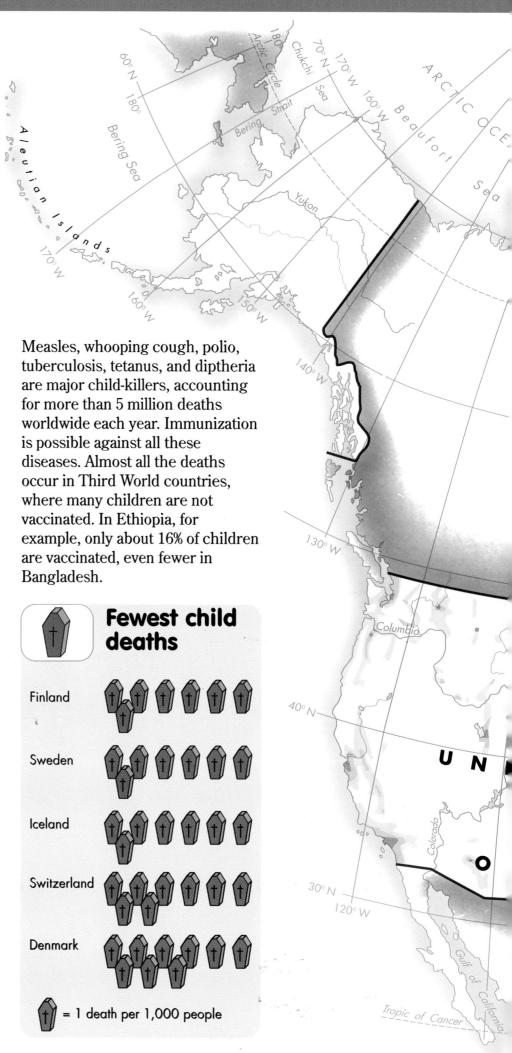

Fewest child deaths

Finland

Sweden

Iceland

Switzerland

Denmark

= 1 death per 1,000 people

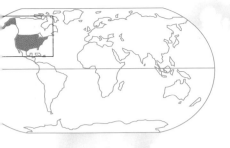

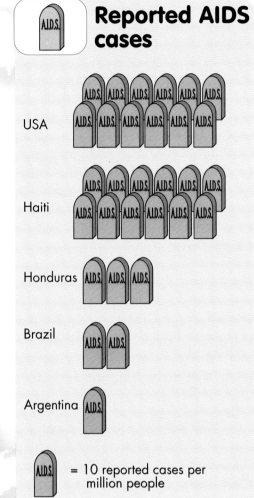

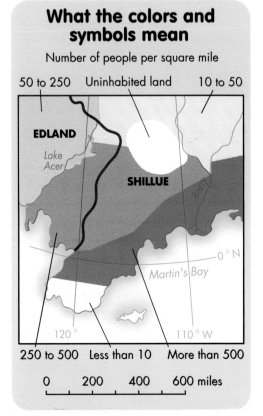

S

epidemic of AIDS continues to
a major toll in human lives and
e a substantial claim on health
resources. By the end of 1989
e than 198,000 cases had been
rted worldwide, with 66% in the
ricas. The epidemic is
easingly affecting the
obean and Central America.

illness is caused by infection
the HIV virus and is
acterized by a long period
een infection and the onset of
otoms of the disease — up to
n or eight years. Cases now
g diagnosed could be the result
al transmission by sexual
act or by use of infected blood
ood products a decade ago.

The World Health Organization
gathers data and reports on cases
of AIDS in an attempt to target
public health programs. In the
Caribbean and some Central
American countries, the pattern
seems to be shifting away from an
illness of men to one that affects
women and children as well.
Women are particularly at risk
because blood transfusions are not
uncommon during childbirth,
especially in countries where
maternal care programs are less
well developed.

The AIDS epidemic in the
Caribbean and Latin America will
stretch health resources. Most
countries give priority to the
survival of women and children
through the provision of
immunization, prenatal education,
and nutrition education.
Predictions from these areas are
that the AIDS epidemic will
severely undermine the gains made
in these health programs.

Reported AIDS cases

USA

Haiti

Honduras

Brazil

Argentina

A.I.D.S. = 10 reported cases per million people

What the colors and symbols mean

Number of people per square mile

50 to 250   Uninhabited land   10 to 50

EDLAND

Lake Acer

SHILLUE

250 to 500   Less than 10   More than 500

0   200   400   600 miles

Asylum

A safe place or refuge from persecution.

Birth control

Techniques used to limit the size of a family. They include contraception, sterilization, and abortion. Birth control is seen as an important means of preventing overpopulation.

Cerebrovascular

Relating to the blood vessels and blood supply of the brain.

Contaminated

Polluted or made impure.

Contraception

Any form of birth control that prevents fertilization of the ovum.

Controversial

An issue or topic about which there is a great deal of argument or debate is said to be controversial, especially if the discussion is carried out in the press or other public forums.

Coronary

Blood vessels, nerves, ligaments, and other parts that surround or encircle a structure, such as the heart.

Degenerative

Causing a decline or deterioration to a lesser state.

Epidemic

Widespread occurrence of a disease that attacks many people in a community at the same time; rapid growth and spread of a disease.

Fertility rate

Fertility is the ability to bear live children. The fertility rate is calculated as the number of births in a year per 1,000 women of reproductive age (generally 15 to 45).

Infant mortality

The number of deaths in the first year of life per 1, children born.

Melanin

The black or dark brown pigments present in the hair, and eyes of humans and animals.

Mortality rate

The death rate. A low mortality rate indicates a lor life expectancy.

Peer group

A social group made up of individuals roughly equ age.

Pharmaceutical

Relating to drugs or the making of drugs.

Propaganda

The organization and distribution of information t either assists or damages a cause.

Sanitation

The supply of clean water and the disposal of sew; for the preservation of public health.

Sterilization

A surgical procedure that leaves a person incapab, producing offspring.

Subsist

To obtain the bare necessities of life.

Urbanization

The migration of rural populations into towns and cities. Urbanization is usually associated with a change from agriculture and cottage industries to mass production and service industries.

Aaseng, Nathan. *Overpopulation.*
New York: Watts, 1991.

Asimov, Issac. *Earth: Our Crowded Spaceship.*
New York: Fawcett, 1978.

Heer, David M. *Society and Population.*
2nd ed. Englewood Cliffs, NJ: Prentice Hall, 1975.

Jeffery, William P. *Unless . . .*
New York: Dodd, Mead, 1975.

Lowenherz, Robert J. *Population.*
Mankato, MN: Creative Education Press, 1970.

McClung, Robert M. *Mice, Moose and Men: How Their Populations
Rise and Fall.*
New York: Morrow, 1973.

Nam, Charles B. *Think About Our Population.*
New York: Walker, 1988.

Stone, A. Harris. Populations: *Experiments in Ecology.*
New York: Watts, 1973.

Stwertka, Eve. *Population: Growth, Change, and Impact.*
New York: Watts, 1981.

Winckler, Suzanne. *Our Endangered Planet: Population Growth.*
Minneapolis, MN: Lerner Publications, 1991.

This index is designed to help you to find places shown on the maps. The index is in alphabetical order and lists all towns, countries, and physical features. After each entry extra information is given to describe the entry and to tell you which country or continent it is in.

The next column contains the latitude and longitude figures. These are used to help locate places on maps. They are measured in degrees. The blue lines drawn across the map are lines of latitude. The equator is at latitude 0°. All lines above the equator are referred to as °N (north of the equator). All lines below the equator are referred to as °S (south of the equator).

The blue lines drawn from the top to the bottom of the map are lines of longitude. The 0° line passes through Greenwich, London, and is known as the Greenwich Meridian. All lines of longitude join the North Pole to the South Pole. All lines to the right of the Greenwich Meridian are referred to as °E (east of Greenwich), and all lines to the left of the Greenwich Meridian are referred to as °W (west of Greenwich).

The final column indicates the number of the page where you will find the place for which you are searching.

If you want to find out where the Gulf of Thailand is, look it up in the alphabetical index. The entry will read:

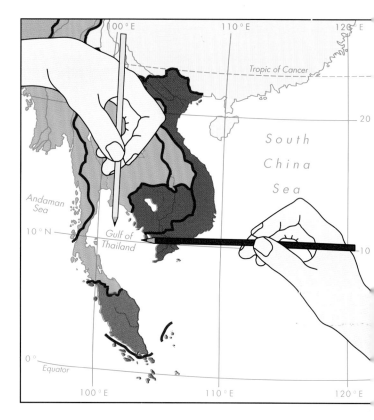

Name, Description	Location		Page
	Lat.	Long.	
Thailand, Gulf of, Asia	11°N	101°E	22

Turn to page 22 in your atlas. The Gulf of Thaila is located where latitude 11°N meets longitude 101 Place a pencil along latitude 11°N. Now take anothe pencil and place it along 101°E. Where the two pen meet is the location of the Gulf of Thailand. Practice finding places in the index and on the maps.

Name, Description	Location		Page
	Lat.	Long.	
A			
Aden, Gulf of, Middle East	12°N	47°E	36
Adriatic Sea, Europe	43°N	15°E	33
Aegean Sea, Greece	35°N	25°E	31
Afghanistan, country in Asia	33°N	65°E	34
Albania, country in Europe	41°N	20°E	31
Aleutian Islands, Alaska	52°N	175°W	40
Algeria, country in Africa	25°N	0°	10
Amazon, river in South America	3°S	56°W	17
Amur, river in Asia	52°N	130°E	29
Andaman Sea, Indian Ocean	11°N	96°E	35
Andorra, country in Europe	43°N	2°E	32
Angola, country in Africa	12°S	18°E	12
Antigua and Barbuda,			
island country in Caribbean Sea	18°N	62°W	15
Arabian Sea, Indian Ocean	18°N	60°E	37
Arafura Sea, Southeast Asia	9°S	135°E	24
Aral Sea, CIS	45°N	60°E	28
Argentina,			
country in South America	40°S	68°W	17
Arkansas, river in United States	35°N	93°W	41
Armenia, country of CIS	40°N	45°E	28

Australia, continent and country	23°S	135°E	2
Austria, country in Europe	48°N	15°E	3
Azerbaijan, country of CIS	40°N	48°E	2
B			
Baffin Bay, North America	72°N	65°W	2
Bahamas,			
island country in Atlantic Ocean	25°N	78°W	1
Bahrain, country in Middle East	26°N	51°E	3
Balikh, river in Middle East	37°N	39°E	3
Balkhash, Lake, Kazakhstan, CIS	46°N	74°E	2
Baltic Sea, Europe	57°N	19°E	2
Bangladesh, country in Asia	23°N	90°E	3
Barbados,			
island country in Caribbean Sea	13°N	59°W	1
Barents Sea, Arctic Ocean	73°N	35°E	2
Bass Strait, Australia	41°S	146°E	2
Beaufort Sea, Arctic Ocean	73°N	140°W	2
Belarus, country of CIS	54°N	28°E	2
Belgium, country in Europe	51°N	5°E	3
Belize, country in Central America	17°N	89°W	1
Bengal, Bay of, Indian Ocean	19°N	89°E	3
Benin, country in Africa	10°N	2°E	1
Bering Sea, Pacific Ocean	60°N	175°W	4

Scott E. Morris an associate professor of geography at the University of Idaho where his current areas of teaching and research interest include mountain geomorphology, field methods, and human impact on the landscape process. Dr. Morris received his Ph.D. from the University of Colorado, Boulder and is published prolifically on the formation and climatic history of mountain landscapes, the effects of wildfire and mineral resource extraction on soil erosion processes, and the influence of water diversion and channel modification on sediment transport.